CAROLYN AVA MARTIN

LLC | BEGINNER'S GUIDE

**Everything on How to Start, Run, and Grow Your First Company Without Prior Experience.
Includes Essential Tax Hacks, Critical Legal Strategies, And Expert Insights**

© Copyright 2024 - All rights reserved.

The content contained within this book may not be reproduced, duplicated, or transmitted without direct written permission from the author or the publisher.

Under no circumstances will any blame or legal responsibility be held against the publisher, or author, for any damages, reparation, or monetary loss due to the information contained within this book. Either direct or indirect. You are responsible for your own choices, actions, and results.

Legal Notice:

This book is copyright protected. This book is only for personal use. You cannot amend, distribute, sell, use, quote, or paraphrase any part of the content within this book. without the consent of the author or publisher.

Disclaimer Notice:

Please note the information contained within this document is for educational and entertainment purposes only. All effort has been executed to present accurate, up-to-date, and reliable complete information No warranties of any kind are declared or implied. Readers acknowledge that the author is not engaging in the rendering of legal, financial, medical, or professional advice. The content within this book has been derived from various sources. Please consult a licensed professional before attempting any techniques outlined in this book.

By reading this document the reader agrees that under no circumstances is the author responsible for any losses, direct or indirect. which are incurred as a result of the use of the information contained within this document, including, but not limited to, – errors. omissions, or inaccuracies

Table of Contents

Introduction 7

Chapter 1: Basics of an LLC 9
    Defining an LLC 9
    Key Features of an LLC 11
    Types of LLCs 16
    Roles within an LLC 17
    Exercise: Assessing if an LLC Suits You 19

Chapter 2: The Formation Process of an LLC 23
    Naming your Business 23
    Registered Agent 26
    Business Address 27
    Articles of Organization 29
    Exercise: Planning Your LLC Formation 32
    Article of Organization Sample Template 34

Chapter 3: Foundations of an LLC 37
    Operating Agreement 37
    Financing Options 43
    Exercises: Mastering the Essentials of Your LLC 47

Chapter 4: Responsibilities of an LLC Owner 49
    Legal Compliance 49
    Documenting Business Activities 51
    Capital Contribution 53
    Workforce Management 54
    Clear and Open Communication 58

Empower Employees 60
Give Recognition and Rewards 60
Strive for Professional Development 61

Chapter 5: The Basics of LLC Taxation 63
The Taxation Process 63
Corporate Taxation 64
Federal, State, and Local Tax Obligations 67
Tax Advantages and Disadvantages of an LLC 68
Strategies for Maximizing LLC's Tax Advantages 69
Hiring a Tax Professional 73
Tax Forms 76
Exercise: Determining your LLC's Taxation 78

Chapter 6: Legal Considerations for Your LLC 81
Personal Liability Protection 81
Legal Disputes and Lawsuits 86
Handling Lawsuits and Disputes 89
Contracts and Agreements 95
Intellectual Property Rights 97
Exercise: Understanding of Legal Considerations ... 101

Chapter 7: Maintaining Compliance 105
Tax Filing 105
Financial Reports 108
Procedures for Tax Filing and Financial Reports 111
Renewing Your LLC 112
Business Licenses and Permits 117
General Tips 119
Exercise: Staying Compliant as an LLC Owner 120

Chapter 8: Evaluating and Managing Risks 123
Types of Risks 123
Risk Assessment 125
Techniques for Managing Risks 126
Insurance Types 127
Financing Growth 128
Exercise: Design a Risk Management Plan 134

Chapter 9: Exit Strategies 137
Reasons to Consider Crafting an Exit Strategy 138
Types of Exit Strategies 139
Mergers and Acquisitions 142
Dissolution 145
Steps to Dissolving Your LLC 146
Deciding the Best Exit Strategy 147
Exercise: What is Your Ideal Exit Strategy? 149
Quiz Results: 151
Exercise: Crafting Your Exit Strategy Plan 151

Conclusion 153

Glossary 155

Resources 159

Exclusive Bonuses 163

Introduction

The world of business offers a myriad of opportunities. From the simplicity of running a lemonade stand to organizing garage sales, the essence of trade can ignite an entrepreneurial spirit. Several individuals balance school and part-time jobs, nurturing the dream of owning their enterprise. Despite many challenges, the aspiration to launch an online venture can motivate individuals to seek independence from traditional corporate life.

In entrepreneurship, navigating the complexity of business formation can be one of the most formidable tasks. As such, it is one thing to conceive a brilliant idea; it is another to transform that concept into a functioning, legally compliant, and profitable business. The journey encompasses understanding different business structures, grappling with legal terminology, managing finances, complying with federal and state regulations, and adapting to ever-changing tax laws. This process can be overwhelming and intimidating.

So, how does one establish a business that ensures financial flexibility, tax benefits, and legal protection while maintaining sanity and guaranteeing success? The answer lies in forming a Limited Liability Company *(LLC)*. This type of business structure merges the benefits of corporations and sole proprietorships while avoiding some of their disadvantages.

This book serves as a comprehensive guide for aspiring entrepreneurs in establishing an LLC. It is grounded in the practical realities of business, and the strategies provided have already helped numerous entrepreneurs establish their LLCs successfully. Likewise, it offers explanations and incorporates various hypothetical scenarios and real-life case studies. These cases involve business owners from all walks of life who have triumphed over obstacles and attained success. Their stories illustrate the potency and efficacy of the strategies offered in this book.

This book is designed to do more than provide information. You will find techniques, tips, and strategies on how to set up, establish, and manage and LLC peppered throughout the entire book. It's intentionally designed this way to serve as your guide along each step of the process. By the end of this book, you will have a comprehensive understanding of every process, requirement, and best practice involved in creating, managing, and maintaining an LLC. Taking action is key to achieving a successful business. Delaying the formation and establishment of an LLC means missing out on potential benefits. *It is time to make your dream business a reality.*

Chapter 1
Basics of an LLC

Starting a business involves decision-making. One crucial decision is choosing the right business structure. This structure is the framework your business operates within. Likewise, this framework will greatly influence ownership, control, liability, and taxes. These factors can impact how successful your business will be and how long it will last.

Among the different business structures, the Limited Liability Company *(LLC)* is a common choice. This chapter contains everything you need to know to start, manage, and maintain your LLC. Understanding this business structure is necessary. As such, you would not want to spend your money, time, and effort on something you do not fully grasp.

Defining an LLC

An LLC blends the most favorable attributes of corporations, partnerships, and sole proprietorships. The *"limited liability"* in its name signifies a key perk— it shields its owners *(referred to as "members")* from personal liability for business-related debts and legal claims. Hence, the members' personal belongings are generally safeguarded if the LLC accumulates debt or faces a lawsuit.

For instance, imagine an LLC that runs a boutique café, Coffee Aroma. It is owned by two friends, Jane and John, who have invested considerable savings to set up this café. They decided to establish their business as an LLC due to the liability protections it offers. One unfortunate day, a customer called Mr. Smith slips on a wet floor in the café and injures himself. Mr. Smith decides to sue Coffee Aroma for his medical expenses, pain, and suffering, claiming negligence on the part of the café for not properly maintaining a safe environment.

As is often the case with personal injury lawsuits, these claims can be expensive. Suppose the court rules in favor of Mr. Smith and awards him a settlement of $200,000. *How does this impact Coffee Aroma and, more importantly, Jane and John?* Here lies the essence of an LLC. Due to the café's LLC structure, Jane and John's liability is *"limited"* to the business's assets. This implies that Mr. Smith can only claim his settlement from Coffee Aroma's business assets. He cannot pursue Jane or John's personal properties.

To compensate Mr. Smith, the owners can instead liquidate the café's business assets to pay the settlement. They can tap into the café's cash reserve or sell equipment and even the business properties if the LLC owns it. In a worst-case scenario, the cafe could be forced into bankruptcy if the business assets are insufficient to cover the settlement. But at least their assets would remain protected.

This protection is a significant advantage, allowing business owners to undertake calculated risks without fearing jeopardizing their wealth. However, this protection is not absolute and can be revoked due to actions we call *"piercing the corporate veil."* Actions and strategies you can do to avoid them will be explained in the later chapter on the legal considerations of an LLC.

Key Features of an LLC

The importance of forming an LLC is not limited to its liability protection. It boasts several unique features that distinguish it from other business entities, such as:

Pass-Through Taxation

Let us say that Cafe Aroma, after paying all the expenses, such as salaries, rent, and supplies, makes a profit of $100,000 at the end of the year.

In some business structures, like corporations, the business would have to pay taxes on this profit first, called *"corporate tax."* Afterward, the remaining profit is distributed to the owners as dividends. The owners will then pay tax on this income on their tax returns, meaning the same money gets taxed twice— a concept known as *"double taxation."*

However, things work differently with an LLC due to its *"pass-through taxation"* feature. The business itself does not pay any tax on the profit. Instead, the profit *"passes through"* the business to the owners. So, in this case, the $100,000 profit would be split between the two owners, each receiving $50,000. They must pay taxes on this profit, which must be reported as income on their tax returns.

So, to simplify, *"pass-through taxation"* results in the business's profits being taxed once— at the individual level rather than the business level. This avoids the *"double taxation"* that happens with corporations and can lead to considerable tax savings for the owners of Coffee Aroma.

Management Flexibility

An LLC's management structure offers a versatile platform adaptable to varying business circumstances and owner preferences. Unlike corporations that must conform to a strict structure with a board of directors, annual shareholder meetings, and careful record-keeping of decision-making processes, LLCs enable owners to choose a management structure that best fits their business needs and level of personal involvement. Options include member-managed or manager-managed setups.

Member-Managed LLC

In this type of management structure, the owners or members participate in the day-to-day operations and decision-making of the business. This option suits businesses where owners want to maintain direct control over operations. In the Coffee Aroma example, if it has a member-managed structure, then Jane and John are hands-on in operating the business.

For instance, they would be directly involved in deciding what goes on the menu. They may taste-test new recipes, consider customer feedback, and observe food trends to make these decisions. Likewise, they would be the ones selecting suppliers. They could also choose local vendors to support the community. Or they might like suppliers based on their products' quality, cost, and reliability.

Regarding marketing strategies, Jane and John would be at the forefront, deciding how to promote their café best. They may brainstorm and execute creative ideas like hosting live music nights, offering seasonal specials, or launching a loyalty rewards program to attract and retain customers.

Appropriateness of a Member-Managed LLC

In our example, the member managers, Jane and John, would own the café and shape its operations, growth, and direction. Entrepreneurs often opt for this structure due to the following:

- **The ability to adapt to small teams.** This structure proves advantageous if staff hiring is difficult, as members can readily assume multiple roles.
- **Expense minimization.** By adopting managerial roles, members save on hiring external managers—a benefit for start-ups or businesses on a budget.
- **Maintaining Strict Control and Monitoring.** This setup allows owners to implement their ideas quickly and make decisions that align with their vision and objectives.

Manager-Managed LLCs

Alternatively, LLCs can be manager-managed, where one or more appointed managers handle the day-to-day operations. In the context of Coffee Aroma, it is possible that Jane and John only want to invest in the café business. They do not want to be involved in managing it, such as hiring staff, ordering supplies, and ensuring compliance with health regulations. In this case, they could hire a professional café manager with the necessary experience and skills to manage these tasks efficiently.

The manager would handle all the daily operations of the café, while Jane and John, as the members, could focus on their roles as investors. The owners may instead be involved in broad strategic decisions— *for instance, whether to open a new branch of the café or invest in a major renovation*— but the manager would handle most of the operational decisions.

Appropriateness of a Manager-Managed LLC

This structure appeals to business owners for several reasons:

- **Streamlining Decision Making.** This structure centralizes authority and responsibility. By assigning decision-making authority to managers, this setup can expedite business operations, eliminating the need for member consultation on every business matter. Thereby avoiding potential delays and facilitating a more efficient decision-making process.
- **Leveraging Expertise.** Members do not always have business management expertise or are inclined to be involved in daily operations. A manager-managed LLC allows skilled professionals to oversee business affairs, leading to better business decisions and healthier profits.
- **Attracting External Investment.** Outside investors often prefer a manager-managed LLC as it shows a clear organizational structure and decision-making hierarchy, reducing ambiguity and enhancing investor confidence.

Profit Distribution

LLCs offer flexibility in profit distribution as they can be tailored to the specific circumstances and agreements of the members. This contrasts sharply with the rigid structure seen in other business structures. For example, the ownership in corporations is split into shares, and each shareholder receives dividends proportionate to the number of shares they own. To give you a clearer picture, a shareholder who owns 20% of the company's shares would receive 20% of the dividends.

However, an LLC operates differently. While members' ownership can be represented as a percentage, how profits and losses are allocated among members isn't strictly tied to these. Instead, members can decide on a different distribution method that may not align with their ownership stakes.

For instance, let us return to our Coffee Aroma example. Suppose Jane owns 70% of the LLC, and John owns 30%. Regardless of this ownership split, they may agree that profits should be divided equally, each receiving 50%. Despite having a smaller ownership stake, John may contribute more to the business in other ways. For example, he may be putting in more work hours or bringing in more customers to compensate for contributing a smaller capital.

Alternatively, they may decide that in the early years of the café, John, who is managing the day-to-day operations, should receive a larger portion of the profits due to greater time commitment. But the profit shares are not fixed and can be adjusted as the business grows and stabilizes.

This kind of arrangement is possible because LLCs allow for what is known as *"special allocations"* in their operating agreement. Special allocations permit the members to distribute profits, losses, and other tax items among the members in a manner different from the percentage of their ownership stake. This is a significant advantage of the LLC structure, as it allows members to structure their profit and loss-sharing agreement best to reflect their contributions to the business and agreed-upon terms. It provides a way for members to reward efforts, recognize contributions, and incentivize certain behaviors in a way that a strict, share-based distribution system like that of corporations does not allow.

Types of LLCs

Having established the flexibility of LLCs, it is important to dive deeper into the distinct types of this business structure you should be aware of. Grasping these different kinds ensures you are well-equipped to manage your LLC effectively, as each variety has unique attributes that influence how your LLC is run and maintained.

- **Single-Member LLC.** The simplest type of LLC since it is owned by just one individual or entity. A single-member LLC is perfect for solo entrepreneurs and small businesses who want to keep their business structure simple while enjoying its benefits.
- **Multi-Member LLC.** A step up from its single-member counterpart, the multi-member LLC opens the door to shared ownership. It brings multiple owners or investors into the equation, making it an ideal structure for collaborative business ventures.

- **Professional LLC (PLLC).** A specialized LLC variant for licensed professionals such as doctors, lawyers, architects, accountants, and others. Some states insist that these professionals form a PLLC instead of a standard LLC, as limited liability protection does not exempt them from responsibilities arising from their professional services or personal duties to clients.
- **Series LLC.** An innovative model that presents the idea of separate *"series"* or *"cells"* within one LLC. Think of it as a beehive, where each series or cell is an individual bee with its responsibilities, resources, and roles, operating independently of the other bees. This groundbreaking structure is allowed in some states and finds particular favor in industries like real estate, where each property can be seen as a different *"bee"* within a real estate Series LLC. Hence, if one property encounters a problem, it does not impact the others, mitigating the risk for the entire Series LLC.

Roles within an LLC

LLCs are versatile, and their roles are as diverse as the businesses that adopt this structure. Given the nuanced complexities arising from its inherent flexibility, understand the various positions within your LLC. There is no universal blueprint since an LLC can function more like a partnership or resemble a corporation's framework. To assist you, below are enumerated potential roles that may need to be filled for a well-functioning LLC.

Member-Owners

At the top of the LLC hierarchy are the owners, often known as members. These individuals are akin to shareholders in a corporation, possessing a share of the LLC proportional to their capital investment. They shape the company's strategic direction and intervene to make decisions.

For example, if a group of friends establishes an LLC to launch a chain of innovative dessert shops, they all become member-owners. They pool their capital, expertise, and resources to kick-start the business, determine matters ranging from shop sites to menu offerings, and split the profits according to their initial contribution.

Managers

As seen in the earlier section about management structure, you can enlist the help of a manager. Either hire an external professional manager or designate one or more members as managers. These individuals are charged with running the business's daily affairs, acting as the company's face to the world, and implementing the decisions taken by the member-owners.

Officers

There can be officers in more complex LLCs, especially those that adopt a corporate-like structure. These positions, often designated as president, vice president, secretary, or treasurer, handle specific areas of the business operation. For example, the president generally acts as the chief executive officer, overseeing all aspects of the company and making key decisions. While the vice president often assumes a supporting role to the president, stepping in when needed and leading specific initiatives or departments. The secretary's role is pivotal in record-keeping, ensuring regulatory compliance, and facilitating communication among members and managers. Lastly, the treasurer, or chief financial officer, oversees the financial and accounting operations of the company, implementing financial strategies and managing budgeting processes.

Employees

The lifeblood of an LLC is its employees. These individuals keep the business running, ensuring the successful delivery of the LLC's products or services. Employee roles can differ widely, contingent upon the industry and the specific business requirements. From customer service agents in a retail LLC to engineers in a tech-focused LLC, these individuals form the company's backbone.

Independent Contractors

Often, an LLC may also engage the services of independent contractors. These professionals are not employees but provide specific services for a defined period. An independent contractor could be a web designer hired to build the company's website, a marketing consultant engaged in launching a new product line, or a lawyer retained to handle legal issues.

Exercise: Assessing if an LLC Suits You

At the end of this chapter, below is an exercise to help you further determine if forming an LLC is the right decision for you and what type, if ever.

- **Define Your Business Objectives**. Clearly outline your business's primary goals and objectives. *What*

do you hope to achieve? How do you envision the growth and development of your business?
- **Understand Your State's Laws.** Research the specific laws and regulations regarding LLCs. *Are there any unique requirements or restrictions you must be aware of?*
- **Risk Assessment.** How much personal risk are you willing to take on in your business? Would you be comfortable with your assets being at risk in the event of business debts or lawsuits? If personal liability is a significant concern for you, an LLC offering limited liability protection might be a good choice.
- **Tax Considerations.** *How do you want your business profits to be taxed? Do you want the profits to be taxed at the business level, or would you prefer them to "pass-through" to your income tax?* LLCs offer pass-through taxation, meaning profits are only taxed once, at the personal level.
- **Evaluate Your Team Composition.** Consider the number of members involved in your business. *Are you a sole owner, or do you have partners or investors?* A single-member LLC could be the right choice if it is just you. If there are multiple owners, a multi-member LLC may be more fitting.
- **Consider Your Management Structure.** Reflect on how you want your business to be managed. A member-managed LLC might be best if the members wish to be hands-on and involved in daily operations. Then, a manager-managed LLC will be a better fit if the members prefer to focus on big-picture decisions and leave the daily tasks to a manager.

- **Future Growth and Investment.** *What are your business plans for future growth and investment? Do you plan to raise capital from investors?* Unlike corporations, LLCs cannot issue shares of stock to attract investors.
- **Professional Guidance.** *Have you considered consulting with a legal or financial advisor to understand the implications of different business structures?* If you need more clarification, it might be beneficial to seek advice from others to make the most informed decision.

Reflecting on these questions can help you determine whether an LLC is the right business structure for your business and decide which type to choose. Remember to take time with your decision and choose wisely since this has long-term implications on liability, taxation, and the daily operations of your business.

Chapter 2

The Formation Process of an LLC

This chapter starts by teaching you how to address the task of choosing a business name. It will also introduce strategies to pick a name that resonates with your target audience and meets all legal requirements.

Subsequently, this chapter will shed light on the critical function of the registered agent—an indispensable player in every LLC. Acting as your official state intermediary, they manage crucial legal and fiscal paperwork.

Finally, you will understand the overall process of filing the articles of organization, the document that officially brings your LLC to life.

Dive in and learn more about the specifics of turning your dreams into a functioning limited liability company.

Naming your Business

In forming an LLC, you need to select a business name. Making a name is not a minor decision or one to be dismissed as a simple task. Likewise, it is not just stringing together words that sound good together. Instead, it is about crafting an identity, a personality, and a brand that will form the foundation of your company's presence in the market.

Picture yourself in a bookstore, scanning the spines of countless books. *Which ones draw your attention? Which ones do you pick up?* Generally, they are the ones that pique your interest and leave a lasting mark. Similarly, your business name is the *"title"* of your company's story. It is the first thing potential clients and customers will notice. The chosen title will imprint on their minds, making it a crucial part of your marketing and branding initiatives.

Consider the tech giant Apple. Nothing about this name screams *'technology.'* It could easily have belonged to a fruit vendor. Yet, when people hear *"Apple,"* their minds leap not to the fruit but to the brand's sleek designs, revolutionary technology, and distinct aesthetic. The same holds for *Amazon*, a name now tantamount to online shopping, despite being borrowed from the world's largest river. These big names have forged a deep bond with their target audiences, reflecting the identities of the companies and gaining iconic status within their sectors.

A well-chosen name can do the same for your LLC. It can infuse your company with a sense of purpose and direction, acting as a compass that points all your business activities toward your goals. Remember to choose a name that reflects your company's essence and communicates its value to your audience.

Legal Rules for LLC Names

The significance of a business name goes beyond marketing and branding. It also bears legal implications. Regulations governing the naming of LLCs vary across different jurisdictions depending on where you will be registering your business. However, amidst these diverse regulations, there remain constant rules you can keep in mind regardless of where you are. These are the following:

Include a Designator

A designator pertains to the specific term in the business name that designates it as an LLC. This could be *"Limited Liability Company," "LLC,"* or *"L.L.C."* Do not forget to add a designator to your business' name as it ensures that anyone interacting with your business is aware of its legal structure and the limited liability protection it provides to its owners.

Steer Clear of Misleading Terms

LLC's name must not contain words that imply it is a different type of business entity. This restriction helps to make sure the actual nature of your business is clear. Assume you are launching a tech start-up and considering the name *"Innovative Solutions Inc. LLC."* Even though this name includes the required "LLC" designator, it also includes "Inc." which could mislead people into thinking your business is a corporation, not an LLC. Therefore, this name could be rejected for not adhering to the rule.

Likewise, be mindful of not using words that can mislead the public into thinking the LLC is a governmental agency. Steer clear from words like *"Federal," "United States," "National,"* or any other terms that could hint at government affiliation.

Name Uniqueness

The name of your business must be unique and not misleadingly similar to any existing entity. Even if your chosen name is not taken, it may not be accepted if it could be easily confused with another business. To illustrate, assume you want to start a digital marketing company. For instance, you initially wish to have a name like "Digital Marketing Masters LLC," which communicates what your business does. However, a registered company, *"Digital Marketing Maestros, LLC," is already* in your jurisdiction. Even though the names are not identical, they are similar enough to potentially cause confusion, which makes your initial choice unacceptable under your jurisdiction's naming rule.

Verifying Name Availability

After finalizing a potential name, the next step is verifying its availability. Most states offer an online database that allows you to search for business names currently in use. The Secretary of State's website or the equivalent department handling business registrations usually has this feature.

For example, if you plan to set up your LLC in Texas, you would visit the Texas Secretary of State's website and navigate to their *"Taxable Entity Search by typing in your desired name"* feature. By typing in your desired name, the system will inform you if it is already in use.

Registered Agent

As you move forward in your LLC formation process, you must appoint a registered agent. Choosing a commendable and trustworthy registered agent is equally essential as naming and branding your business.

A registered agent is a person or business entity you appoint when setting up your LLC and will continue to rely on during your operation. Their primary job is to receive vital legal and tax documents for your business. It is necessary because the state needs a reliable communication method with your LLC. Whether to send annual reports or tax documents or to notify your business about a lawsuit *(also known as service of process),* the state will send these documents to your registered agent.

Imagine a supplier accuses your LLC of contract violation and opts for legal recourse. The court would send the lawsuit papers to your registered agent. Without a registered agent, you risk missing the lawsuit notification. This oversight could lead to a court decision in your absence, possibly inflicting significant repercussions on your business.

The role of a registered agent is not just limited to accepting lawsuit papers. They also receive other vital state notifications, such as reminders to file annual reports or updates regarding changes in state business laws.

Business Address

Another element in the formation process of an LLC is the business address. This address serves as the official location of your company. It is used for a variety of reasons. For instance, it is where you primarily receive your business mail not served to your registered agent and where your business records are usually kept. Besides that, the address is generally used in marketing materials, invoices, contracts, and other public-facing documents.

More than just a mailbox, it is also where your business is legally recognized to exist. This business addresses a fundamental part of your business identity and the place where your business officially *'lives.'* That's why it's important to choose an address that meets your state's requirements and aligns with your needs and the image you want to project to the public. For example, suppose you are launching a high-end fashion design business and making it an LLC. Let us say you select an address in a well-known fashion district of a major city, like the Garment District in New York City. This location is synonymous with fashion and design and can positively impact your brand image. It suggests your business is at the heart of the fashion industry, which can help attract high-end clientele and industry professionals.

Selecting the Right Business Address

When choosing a business address for your LLC, there are some considerations to remember.

Depending on the specific regulations in your state, *a P.O. Box may not be accepted as a business address.* Typically, an actual physical address is required. This could be a commercial office location, or in many states, it could also be a residential address.

For instance, if you are a small business owner starting an LLC from home, you may *use your home address as your business address*. However, you should be aware that doing so will make this information public record. It will be accessible to anyone who searches for your LLC's details. This could concern those who prefer to keep their home address private. Alternatively, if you run a business that requires a commercial space like a retail store or a restaurant, then your business address would typically be the location of this space.

Other options exist for those who prefer not to use their home address or if a physical business location is not applicable. As such, consider *renting a mailbox* from a private company that provides a real street address, not a P.O. Box number. Doing so can create a separation between your personal and business correspondence. Another option is a *virtual office service* that provides a physical business address and additional services like mail forwarding.

Articles of Organization

Establishing an LLC reaches fruition only when you file the articles of organization. This essential document signifies the official inception of your business in the eyes of your state. Once filed and accepted by your state, they serve as the official record of your LLC's formation and its agreed-upon operating structure. Not merely a certification document, it is a legally binding contract between the LLC's members and the state detailing their commitments to the LLC and its operation.

Moreover, it offers proof of your LLC's existence, contributing to transparency about your business's structure and authenticity. The document is typically accessible to the public once filed, providing transparency about your business's structure and legitimacy. This can build trust with potential clients, customers, and partners who can verify your LLC's existence and learn about its structure.

Specifics of the Articles of Organization

While the specifics of articles might vary according to your state's distinct requirements, it generally includes the following key information:

- **The official name and address of your LLC.** This label and location set the identity of your business.

- **Registered agent's name and address.** The registered agent handles critical legal and tax documents on your LLC's behalf.
- **LLC's purpose.** This section outlines what your business plans to do. Some states require a specific business objective, whereas others may accept a more generic purpose.
- **LLC's management structure.** Specify in this section if your LLC will be managed by its members or a manager.
- **The names of the initial members or managers.** Depending on your selected management structure, you must enlist the names of either the initial members or the managers.

Filing the Articles of Organization

Once done preparing your articles of organization, submit them to the relevant state agency, typically the Secretary of State. Below is a general walkthrough of the process.

1. **Prepare the Document.** Start by filling out the document with all the necessary information. Usually, it includes details about your LLC's name, business address, registered agent, purpose, management structure, and initial members or managers. Some states may have additional requirements; research what is needed.
2. **Review Your Document.** After filling out your articles of organization, reviewing them thoroughly is essential. Check for any errors or omissions. Remember, this document is a legal contract between

your LLC and the state, and any inaccuracies could lead to issues.

3. **File the Document.** Once everything in your Articles of Organization is accurate and complete, file it. The filing process varies from state to state. Some states allow for online filing, while others require you to mail in the document. Find the necessary instructions and forms on your Secretary of State website.

4. **Settle the Filing Fee.** Filing the articles of organization usually comes with a fee. The amount can vary greatly depending on the state, ranging from $50 to several hundred dollars. Note that this fee is often non-refundable, even if your filing is not accepted, so double-check everything before you file.

5. **Wait for Approval.** After submitting your articles of organization and paying the filing fee, the state will review your document. If everything is in order, your LLC will be officially registered. The state usually sends a confirmation document, such as a Certificate of Formation or a similar document, as proof that your LLC has been legally formed.

6. **Create an Operating Agreement.** While not always required to be filed with the state, an Operating Agreement is highly recommended for all LLCs. This internal document outlines the ownership and operating procedures of the LLC, providing a clear framework for how the business will be run. Preparing this around the same time you file your articles of organization is a good idea.

Though the process may seem straightforward, approach the articles of organization with care. Errors or omissions could lead to delays or, worse, legal issues down the road. Investing time and resources upfront is better than facing potential headaches later. Remember, this process does not have to be navigated alone. Consider enlisting the help of a business advisor or attorney to guide you through the process, ensuring every box is ticked and every requirement is met. After all, the journey of building a business is a significant one, and it is a journey that is often best traveled with the support of experienced guides.

Exercise: Planning Your LLC Formation

Now that you have learned about forming an LLC, let us break it into actionable steps. This exercise will help you plan and understand the tasks at hand. Remember, it is fine if you are still getting ready to finalize some decisions; the goal is to get you thinking and planning.

1. **Drafting Potential Business Names.** Consider what you want your business to represent and who your target audience is. With that in mind, draft a list of five potential names for your LLC. Remember, a good business name is unique, memorable, and reflects your brand.
2. **Researching State-Specific Rules.** Look up the specific rules for LLC names in your state. Write down the key requirements, focusing particularly on elements that will affect your choice of business name.

3. **Checking Name Availability.** Choose your top three names from your list. Use the online database provided by your state to check the availability of these names. Take note of the results.
4. Identifying Your Registered Agent. Consider who you want to act as your LLC's registered agent. Write down why they would fit this role well.
5. **Understanding the Articles of Organization.** Visit your state's Secretary of State website and download a sample form or template for the articles of organization. Go through each section, making sure you understand what information is required. I also included a sample template at the end of this chapter, so you can also check that out.
6. **Reflecting on the Process.** Reflect on what you learned and done so far. *Do you feel more prepared to start your LLC? What parts of the process are still unclear?* Write down any questions or concerns, and consider contacting a business advisor or attorney to discuss them.

With this exercise, you have a clearer picture of what lies ahead in your journey to forming an LLC.

Article of Organization Sample Template

Articles of Organization

Article I
Name

The name of the company is _____

_____

Article II
Duration

The term of duration for this company shall be: _____.

Article III
Purpose

The purpose for which this company is organized is to conduct any lawful business pursuant to state statute _____, including but not limited to:

_____

_____

_____

Article IV
Registered Agent

The name and address of the company's initial registered agent:

_____

_____

The company maintains in its records the statement of acceptance by the registered agent.

Article V
Principal Office & Mailing Address

The principal office of the company is located at: _____

The mailing address of the company is: _____

Article VI
Members

The names and addresses of members are as follows:

_____

_____

Article VII
Management

The name(s) and address(es) of the individual(s) responsible for the day-to-day operations of the company are as follows:

_____

_____

Article VIII
Capital Contributions

The total amount of cash contributed to the company: _____

Description and agreed value of property contributed to the company:

Property	Value
_____	_____
_____	_____
_____	_____

Article IX
Additional Contributions

The total of additional contributions agreed to be made by all members and the times at which or the events upon the happening of which they will be made:

Description of Contribution	Member Name

Due Date _____

_____	_____
_____	_____
_____	_____

Article X
Liability

The members of the company are not personally liable for the acts or debts of the company.

Article XI
Other Provisions

Additional provisions the members elect to set out in these Articles are:

_____

_____

_____

I, _____, acting as the Organizer for this company, execute these Articles of

Organization dated this ____ day of _____, _____.

_____
Signature of Organizer

Chapter 3
Foundations of an LLC

With your LLC officially established, your business journey truly begins. Establishing a robust foundation is paramount to ensure the smooth operation and potential growth of your business. Central to this is writing an operating agreement and funding your company.

Operating Agreement

The operating agreement serves as the cornerstone of your LLC. It outlines how your business will operate, detailing member responsibilities, clarifying the management structure, and outlining procedures for key business operations. Moreover, it helps avoid potential conflicts and ensures smooth business operations. This section entails the importance and components of the operating agreement.

Operating Agreement vs. Articles of Organization

At first, you may find operating agreements and articles of organization similar. However, they serve unique purposes and contain different information, even though they are essential to forming an LLC.

Think of the articles of organization as your LLC's birth certificate. This public document, filed with the state, officially marks the birth of your business. It offers basic details about your LLC, such as its name, business address, and the name and address of the registered agent. Occasionally, it also contains the names of the members and managers.

In contrast, the operating agreement is your LLC's internal rulebook. It is a private document and is not typically required to be filed with the state. It goes into far more detail than the articles of organization, outlining how the business will be run, the members' rights and responsibilities, voting power, the process for admitting new members, profit and loss distribution, and procedures for dissolution, among others. Lastly, it provides a roadmap for decision-making processes and is instrumental in preventing and resolving potential disputes among members.

Contents of the Operating Agreement

Serving as the foundational guideline, the operating agreement directs the functional and financial decision-making processes within the LLC. More than a mere formality, it is the operational blueprint that outlines the rights and responsibilities of the members, dictates the profit and loss distribution, and provides a roadmap for conflict resolution and potential dissolution scenarios.

With the flexibility to be tailored to the business's specific needs, it can potentially prevent misunderstandings and foster a harmonious working environment. From determining the management structure to stipulating procedures for member exits and new admissions, the contents of the operating agreement form the cornerstone of an effective and efficient LLC.

Some things to include in your LLC's operating agreement include the following:

Management Structure

Although prior chapters have explored various management structures, it remains vital to emphasize your selected approach within this document. The operating agreement serves as a comprehensive guide that delineates roles and responsibilities, ensuring each member within the organization is aware of their specific tasks and associated expectations. By formally detailing this structure, it promotes transparency and fosters accountability. Ultimately contributes to the seamless operation of the company.

Allocation of Profits and Losses

The distribution of profits and losses is an integral attribute of a Limited Liability Company *(LLC)* and necessitates meticulous detailing within the operating agreement. It is incumbent upon the members to delineate the proportions of profit and loss allocation, reflecting a consensus reached after careful deliberation. A rational and equitable plan for the distribution not only promotes transparency and mutual goodwill among the members but also establishes clear financial expectations within the confines of the LLC. This full-bodied structure, built on equity and clarity, will foster a professional and harmonious business environment.

Capital Contributions

Defining each member's initial investment must also be included in the operating agreement. It is about more than just stating the figures, though. Provisions must be made for scenarios where the business may require additional financial funding. For instance, the agreement could specify mechanisms for members to contribute more capital or for the LLC to raise external funding.

Moreover, *what happens if a member falls short of their capital commitment?* Your operating agreement should articulate the consequences—*could they lose a part of their ownership share or their voting rights?* Setting these guidelines from the onset can prevent potential conflicts and ensure a smoother operational course for your LLC.

Voting Procedures

An LLC is not a dictatorship but a system where members' voices matter. The operating agreement should amplify these voices by clearly outlining the voting rights of members. A coin toss may work for a football game, but you will need a more thought-out mechanism in your operating agreement. Be clear as possible and include answers to questions like whether each member gets one vote or their voting power corresponds to their ownership percentage. *How many votes are required to pass a decision—is it a simple majority, a supermajority, or unanimous consent? And what about tiebreakers?*

Transfer of Ownership

Transferring LLC ownership is not just about swapping names on paperwork. It is a delicate process that requires careful consideration and a thorough understanding of your operating agreement. It should outline the specific process for ownership transfer. Key points often include:

- **Rights of First Refusal.** This provision gives existing members the first chance to buy shares or interests when another member wants to sell. Thus, allowing current members to maintain control over who owns the business and prevent unwanted third-party involvement.

- **Approval Process.** Generally, the transfer of ownership in an LLC requires approval from the existing members. Often, this approval takes the form of a majority vote, but the specifics can depend on the operating agreement.
- **Valuation.** The agreement should unambiguously define how to determine the ownership interest's value during a sale, transfer, or a member's exit. This usually involves a business valuation expert or a predetermined formula. Having a set method for valuation helps ensure fairness and transparency when ownership stakes are being bought, sold, or otherwise changed, protecting the interests of all members.

Unforeseen Circumstances

A good operating agreement also anticipates unexpected situations:

- **Member Death.** What happens to a member's stake upon their demise?
- **Bankruptcy.** How is the ownership interest handled if a member declares bankruptcy?
- **Divorce.** How does a member's divorce impact their share of the LLC?

Dissolution

All good ventures may eventually conclude, including your Limited Liability Company *(LLC)*. It is not an agreeable contemplation, but it necessitates prudent deliberation. The operating agreement should specify the protocols for a structured and efficient dissolution of the LLC. As such, it involves identifying circumstances prompting dissolution, such as a resolution passed by members or attaining particular business objectives.

The agreement should also clearly state the methodology for distributing assets amongst members and the plan for addressing outstanding liabilities. In-depth planning in this respect can facilitate an elegant and orderly closure, safeguarding the members' interests throughout the final phase of the LLC's existence.

Dispute Resolution

In business, it is an acknowledged reality that even the most harmonious partnerships may encounter disagreements from time to time. Limited Liability Company *(LLC)* members are not immune to such situations. When these disagreements escalate into disputes, they can impact the functionality and stability of the business negatively. This is the juncture where the operating agreement demonstrates its integral role, acting as a mediator to restore equilibrium.

Incorporating a dispute resolution clause into your operating agreement can prove invaluable when the conflict begins to fall. As such, it establishes a comprehensive and unequivocal procedure for resolving disputes, suggesting a pathway that includes negotiation, mediation, or arbitration. The primary objective of this clause is to facilitate an amicable and expeditious resolution of issues. Thereby circumventing the potentially extensive financial implications associated with litigation.

Financing Options

There are various avenues to secure funding for your LLC, each with its benefits and caveats, some of these are the following:

Self-funding

Self-funding, or *bootstrapping*, is often the first option on the funding journey. This route allows you to maintain total control over your LLC, avoiding any dilution of equity or obligation to lenders. Here are the self-funding options you can utilize:

Personal Savings

Many entrepreneurs depend on personal savings for the primary investment in their Limited Liability Company *(LLC)*. This funding method provides complete autonomy and versatility. Nevertheless, it does present substantial risk, as it could deplete one's financial safety net. Should the venture fail, financial recovery might be demanding. While personal savings can be a funding source, entrepreneurs must assess their financial risks meticulously. Likewise, they must ensure a sufficient safety net remains intact for personal necessities.

Retirement Accounts

Certain entrepreneurs might consider allocating funds from their retirement accounts toward their LLC. This route, although higher in risk, can be explored cautiously under the guidance of a professional financial advisor due to potential early withdrawal penalties and tax repercussions that could significantly influence one's financial trajectory.

Home Equity

Homeowners with considerable equity may consider securing a home equity line of credit as a funding mechanism for their LLC. This approach can provide substantial capital. However, it involves placing your residence as collateral, which could be in jeopardy if the enterprise fails.

Loans and Grants

When self-funding proves insufficient or unsuitable, loans and grants offer credible alternatives for funding. These avenues generally necessitate rigorous applications and adherence to stipulations.

Bank Loans

Conventional bank loans can furnish substantial capital for your LLC. Acquiring such a loan requires a strong business proposal, a solid credit history, and occasionally collateral. While the interest rates can be comparatively low, mandatory repayments could strain your business's cash flow if financial performance fails to meet expectations.

SBA Loans

The U.S. Small Business Administration (SBA) offers various loan programs for small businesses. SBA loans usually have more accessible qualification criteria than traditional bank loans, offering lower interest rates and extended repayment terms. However, the application process can be time-consuming and may require extensive documentation.

Grants for Small Businesses

Grants provide non-repayable funding, often tied to specific industries, demographics, or business objectives. Although securing a grant can be competitive and necessitates meeting specific criteria, it is a valuable avenue to explore. Entrepreneurs are encouraged to investigate local, state, and federal grant opportunities.

Investors and Equity

Attracting investors can be a crucial strategy for businesses, including LLCs, when they need significant financial resources to grow, innovate, or survive. They provide substantial capital enabling you to undertake large projects, expand operations, or weather financial difficulties without requiring immediate payback or interest payments as a traditional loan would.

Though directly selling ownership stakes in your LLC is a way to generate funds, investors often require equity in exchange for their investment. This equity signifies a share of ownership in the company, granting the investor a slice of the profits and, in some instances, voting rights in key company decisions. This varies from lenders like banks, offering loans to be repaid with interest but not claiming an ownership stake in the company.

Besides reducing your share of future profits, this dilution might curb your control over the business, particularly if the equity comes with voting rights. If you relinquish a 20% equity stake to an investor from your 100% owned LLC, you now hold 80% of your company. This means the investor might also command 20% of the voting rights.

That being said, remember that equity dilution represents a trade-off. You gain access to capital necessary for business growth but give up some ownership, profit sharing, and potential control. Thus, evaluate the necessity of external funding thoroughly, the credentials of the investor, and the potential impacts of dilution on your future stake. Lastly, control the business before deciding to take on an equity investment.

Angel Investors

Angel investors are high-net-worth individuals who provide capital for start-ups or nascent enterprises, typically in return for equity ownership. This group of investors generally offers terms more advantageous than other lenders. Besides that, they tend to support ventures that align with their interests or areas of expertise.

Venture Capitalists (VCs)

Venture capitalists represent firms that make significant financial investments in high-growth companies exhibiting substantial potential. In addition to providing capital, VCs often contribute strategic guidance, mentorship, and beneficial industry connections. They usually acquire a large equity stake and actively participate in strategic decisions. To secure a return on their investment, venture capitalists frequently advocate for quick growth and effective exit strategies.

Private Equity (PE) Firms

Private equity firms provide capital and expertise, often executing strategic modifications to enhance a company's value. They can supply the resources necessary to drive considerable growth or facilitate extensive restructuring efforts. However, the primary objective of PE firms is to maximize profits from their investments, which may not always align with a company's long-term objectives.

Crowdfunding

Crowdfunding is a method of raising capital that involves soliciting small financial contributions from a large pool of individuals, generally facilitated through online platforms. As such, it can be reward-based, where contributors receive a product or service in exchange for their donation. Conversely, it can also be equity-based, in which contributors receive shares in the company. While crowdfunding can effectively raise capital, it requires significant marketing efforts and careful planning. Furthermore, raising substantial funds may prove challenging. Hence, if the fundraising target is not reached, the company may walk away with no funds at all.

Exercises: Mastering the Essentials of Your LLC

In this exercise, the perspective of a member within a Limited Liability Company (LLC) is assumed, aiming to construct a plausible operating agreement. Subsequently, exploration and evaluation of various financing alternatives for the envisioned business expansion are undertaken, weighing their advantages and potential drawbacks.

Part 1: Understanding Operating Agreements

1. Imagine being a member of a new LLC called *"TechFuture Innovations."* This LLC is formed by five

members who each bring different skills and financial contributions to the table.

- Draft an outline of an operating agreement for TechFuture Innovations. Highlight key elements such as member roles and responsibilities, distribution of profits and losses, adding or removing members, and protocols for resolving internal disputes.
- Discuss how the operating agreement can evolve and the process for amendments.

Part 2: Exploring Financing Options

1. TechFuture Innovations plans to launch a new line of eco-friendly tech products and is looking for financing options to fund this new venture.

    - List and describe at least three financing options the LLC can utilize.
    - Discuss each financing option's potential advantages and drawbacks, considering aspects such as control over decision-making, financial risk, and potential impact on the LLC's operations.

Understanding these elements equips entrepreneurs to make sound decisions.

Chapter 4
Responsibilities of an LLC Owner

From legal compliance and capital contribution to high-stakes decision-making and workforce management, every aspect of your business depends on you. Understanding the responsibilities tied to your role can empower you to drive your business toward unprecedented success.

Legal Compliance

The scope of legal responsibilities is extensive; however, this discourse will primarily focus on compliance with federal and state-specific regulations. Adherence to these rules necessitates a proactive approach toward comprehending and implementing the relevant laws associated with your Limited Liability Company *(LLC)*. Neglecting these responsibilities could result in grave consequences, including the imposition of fines, penalties, and potential legal proceedings, which could endanger the reputation and success of your business.

While diverse, these regulations converge toward a common goal of ensuring legal and ethical business practices. They serve as the guiding principles that your business is obligated to follow. These laws and rules protect all involved parties— *owners, employees, customers, and other stakeholders*—by fostering a business environment characterized by fairness, transparency, and accountability. Following these reinforces your LLC's commitment to ethical business conduct, bolstering its reputation and credibility in the marketplace.

Federal Laws

At the federal level, several laws impact the operation of an LLC. Some of these are listed below.

- **Tax Laws.** The Internal Revenue Service *(IRS)* governs federal tax regulations for LLCs. These laws dictate the tax obligations of your LLC and the specific manner in which taxes should be filed.
- **Employment Laws.** Should your LLC have employees, federal employment laws apply. These include the Fair Labor Standards Act *(FLSA)*, outlining minimum wage and overtime pay, and the Occupational Safety and Health Act *(OSHA)*, ensuring safe working conditions.
- **Privacy Laws.** If your LLC handles personal data, it must comply with federal privacy laws, including the Federal Trade Commission and Privacy Acts.

State Regulations

In parallel, LLC owners must also adhere to state-specific regulations. States have distinct regulations, with the complexity of these laws varying widely. Some states require LLCs to submit an annual report and pay a corresponding fee, while others do not impose such requirements. Certain states enforce stricter regulations on LLCs operating in specific sectors like healthcare or finance.

Documenting Business Activities

Expanding upon the obligations of a Limited Liability Company *(LLC)* owner, one duty requiring considerable diligence and accuracy is the upkeep of records and reporting. Likewise, this task is the foundation of a powerful, transparent, and legally abiding enterprise. Neglecting the importance of meticulous record-keeping can precipitate formidable obstacles and complications, particularly in administering fiscal matters, legal responsibilities, and business expansion.

Proper documentation is indispensable to operating any business where fiscal and legal transparency is paramount. The records **provide a snapshot of your business's financial health,** aiding in effective decision-making and strategic planning. They can offer insights into your income and expenses, allowing you to identify growth opportunities and potential issues affecting your company's profitability.

In addition to helping you keep track of your business performance, well-maintained records also **fulfill a legal requirement.** LLCs are required by law to maintain certain records for a stipulated period. They facilitate accurate tax filing and ensure you're ready for potential audits from authorities. Detailed records can also be valuable in legal scenarios, providing the necessary documentation to support your case.

Record keeping also plays a pivotal role when **seeking external financing.** For instance, having orderly and accurate records can demonstrate your business's financial stability and growth potential when applying for a business loan or attracting investors. They can instill confidence in potential lenders and investors and give you an edge in a competitive business environment.

Remember, **record keeping is not a mere administrative task** but a vital responsibility that impacts various aspects of your business. Ensuring you meet this obligation will streamline your operations, keep you compliant with regulations, and facilitate your strategic planning and decision-making processes.

Types of Records to Keep

The particular records one must maintain may be contingent upon the nature of one's business. However, several categories of records are universally relevant to most business entities.

- **Financial Records.** Undoubtedly, these are the most imperative records to maintain. They give you an overview of your financial standing and are crucial for filing taxes. These include profit and loss statements, balance sheets, and cash flow statements.
- **Legal Documents.** Documents like the operating agreement, articles of organization, and business permits are examples of legal documents. Organizing them is critical to ensuring legal compliance and protection for your business, as you can easily access them in case you need them.
- **Tax Records.** Beyond the financial paperwork for tax filings, this group also encompasses your filed tax returns and any associated evidence. Retaining these records for at least three years is advisable, giv-

en that the IRS can audit your business within this timeframe.
- **Employee Records.** If you have employees, you need to keep comprehensive records for each one. These should include their application and resume, employment contract, records of salary and benefits, performance evaluations, and any disciplinary actions.
- **Business Operations and Meeting Records.** This category covers records such as minutes of meetings, annual reports, and any changes to your operating agreement. Maintaining these records can prove helpful when making business decisions or resolving disputes.

Capital Contribution

Think of your LLC as a growing tree— your dream that needs sustenance to flourish. The capital contribution is the life-giving water that nourishes this tree, making it strong and enabling it to bear fruit. As an LLC owner, one of your responsibilities is to ensure this nourishment is aptly provided.

Capital contribution refers to the amount of money or assets you invest into your LLC. It is the financial foundation upon which your business is built and grows. This initial contribution becomes the operating capital for your LLC's day-to-day expenses and long-term investments. I have discussed earlier the different financing options you can use. But remember, this is not a one-and-done scenario. As your LLC evolves, so will its financial needs. For instance, reinvest profits, inject more personal funds, or even bring in additional members to meet the growing needs of your enterprise.

Thus, a capital contribution is not a static responsibility but an ongoing commitment that changes with your business's lifecycle.

However, your contribution to the LLC's capital is not only about money. It can also be in assets like property, equipment, or intellectual property. Note that the value of these contributions directly influences your ownership stake in the LLC. The more you contribute, the greater your ownership share. Unless otherwise stipulated in the operating agreement.

Ensuring adequate capitalization can also shield you from personal liability. If your LLC is undercapitalized, creditors could pierce the corporate veil, holding you personally liable for the company's debts. Hence, capital contribution does not merely fuel your business's growth; it also fortifies your protection as an LLC owner.

Remember, your role as an LLC owner is not just about making the initial capital contribution; it is about nurturing your business with continuous financial support and strategic reinvestment.

Workforce Management

Further to the discussion on the obligations of a Limited Liability Company *(LLC)* owner, personnel management is an essential responsibility that commands significant consideration. As the proprietor of an LLC, you can either employ full-time staff members or enlist the expertise of independent contractors. Each of these options presents unique implications for your enterprise and could influence the operational flexibility of your business. Thus, the decision must be carefully evaluated: *Will your enterprise thrive on the regular rhythm provided by full-time employees? Or would it benefit from the versatile tempo of independent contractors contributing their unique skills?* This strategic selection is bound to influence the trajectory of your LLC.

Permanent Employees

These are individuals hired by the LLC under an employment contract. They work under the company's control, adhering to company-set schedules, procedures, and guidelines.

On the positive side, having permanent employees can lead to a more stable and cohesive team. Employees can contribute to a company's culture and become integral to its growth and success. This sense of continuity and commitment can translate into improved customer service and a deeper understanding of your business operations.

However, the flip side involves more responsibilities for the business owner. As such, there will be a need to manage payroll taxes, comply with labor and employment laws, offer benefits, and handle other administrative tasks. Moreover, you may be held accountable for your employees' actions during their employment, adding to your legal responsibilities.

Independent Contractors

Contrarily, independent contractors are autonomous entities or businesses the LLC engages for designated tasks or projects. They retain more control over their professional obligations, such as determining their work schedule and executing their tasks per their preferred methodology. Independent contractors bear their tax obligations but are not privy to employee benefits.

The engagement of independent contractors can provide enhanced flexibility and cost efficiency. This arrangement allows for more effective cost control, given that remuneration is directly linked to work performed. Additionally, the burden of tax-related administrative tasks lies with the contractor, thereby lightening your operational load.

However, this modality does come with its own set of drawbacks. Independent contractors exhibit less predictability. Besides, their loyalty and commitment toward your business do not parallel that of full-time employees. Misclassifying an employee as an independent contractor can lead to legal and financial repercussions. It is imperative to adhere strictly to the guidelines laid down by the Internal Revenue Service *(IRS)* about worker classification.

Making the Right Choice

The choice between hiring permanent employees or independent contractors is not a one-size-fits-all decision. It hinges on various factors, including the nature of the work, the degree of control desired, budget considerations, and the level of risk you are willing to accept. For instance, an LLC running a software development firm may hire permanent employees for long-term projects, ensuring stability and a steady workforce.

While a marketing LLC can hire an independent contractor for a short-term branding campaign, providing the company with specialized expertise without a long-term commitment. As seen in the examples, if control, stability, and a dedicated workforce are important to you, then hiring employees might be the best route. However, if flexibility, cost-efficiency, and access to a wider talent pool are preferred, working with independent contractors may be more advantageous.

Steps to Hiring Employees

The precise timing of employee recruitment can significantly influence the trajectory of a business. Engaging new staff prematurely could deplete financial resources. Meanwhile, delaying hiring may result in missed growth opportunities or an overwhelmed existing team. To assist in navigating this, here is a systematic approach to employee recruitment:

- **Identify the need for additional staff.** As a general guideline, consider engaging more employees when your current team's workload becomes overly taxing or when additional competencies are required for business expansion. Continuously assess your business to seize the right recruitment timing.
- **Start the recruitment process.** Upon identification of the hiring requirement, commence the process by generating a comprehensive job description. This description should accurately delineate the role's duties, the skills demanded, and what prospective employees can anticipate from the position. After finalizing the job description, advertise the vacancy on appropriate platforms, including job boards and social media, contingent upon the probable location of your target applicants.

- **Select the candidates.** This process encompasses several stages: *evaluating received applications, conducting interviews with potential candidates, and performing background checks.* Remember that the selection process aims to identify a candidate who can contribute sustainable value to your company. For instance, if you were the proprietor of a café chain intending to expand, you would not simply hire more baristas. Instead, you would seek individuals possessing customer service skills, an enthusiasm for coffee, and a willingness to learn, as these traits would ensure that the new employees could foster the company's growth and maintain its customer-centric ethos.

Strategies for Effective Management and Leadership

Leadership transcends the confines of a mere organizational role; *it is a mindset requiring the capacity to galvanize, steer, and inspire a team toward common objectives.* The bedrock of impactful leadership and management is cultivating a nurturing environment that promotes progress, facilitates open communication, and acknowledges achievements. These vital components metamorphose the work setting and drive the team toward greater success and productivity.

Clear and Open Communication

Successful leadership is intrinsically contingent upon the adept execution of communication. It extends beyond mere dispensing information, emphasizing establishing a transparent dialogue that fosters feedback and engenders comprehension. Given the escalating diversity of modern workplaces and the ubiquity of remote work modalities, open communication is indispensable for ensuring that each team member feels acknowledged, valued, and engaged.

The institution of unambiguous and open communication necessitates the establishment of a culture wherein every individual's voice carries significance. It is incumbent upon leaders to communicate expectations, institute transparent metrics of performance, and disseminate the objectives and strategic directions of the company. This may be facilitated through periodic meetings, disseminated newsletters, or electronic mail updates.

Moreover, it is imperative to cultivate a secure environment for employees to express their thoughts, apprehensions, and feedback. This may involve the implementation of open-door policies, the introduction of suggestion boxes, or the establishment of systems for anonymous feedback. Furthermore, leaders ought to exhibit receptivity to feedback, manifesting their appreciation for a multitude of perspectives and their readiness to initiate requisite alterations.

Capitalizing on technology to bolster effective communication is of paramount importance, particularly in the context of remote work. Digital tools, such as video conferencing, instant messaging, and project management platforms, can significantly augment the transparency and inclusivity of communication.

Empower Employees

Empowerment is about entrusting your employees with responsibilities and decision-making authority, reinforcing their significance within the organization. When employees feel empowered, they are more likely to take ownership of their work, be proactive, and strive for better results.

However, empowerment does not imply relinquishing control. Instead, it is about creating a balanced environment where employees can make decisions within defined boundaries. It involves providing them with the necessary resources, support, and autonomy to execute their tasks effectively. This decision-making power can stimulate creativity, initiative, and a sense of ownership. Give regular feedback to guide employees in decision-making and ensure their efforts align with company goals.

Give Recognition and Rewards

Recognizing and appreciating your team's efforts boost morale, increase productivity, and enhance job satisfaction. Acknowledging their contributions to your organization's accomplishments sends a message of appreciation. Such recognition could be as simple as a heartfelt *"thank you"* during a team gathering, a mention in an organizational update, or even tangible rewards like bonuses or advancements.

To construct an effective recognition and reward system, outline clear and quantifiable performance measures. These guidelines allow everyone to understand what represents outstanding work. Regularly celebrate the small victories along with larger achievements. This could mean a public commendation during a meeting or an appreciative email. Likewise, tailor your praises, recognizing the unique contributions of each team member. For substantial achievements, contemplate tangible rewards such as bonuses, gift cards, additional time off, or potential advancements.

Nevertheless, fairness should be your compass in this process. Ensure the rewards and acknowledgments are based on merit rather than favoritism. Timely recognition is equally vital; prompt appreciation for a well-done job resonates more powerfully than delayed recognition. Lastly, consider fostering peer recognition, where team members can acknowledge each other's efforts. This strategy not only cultivates a positive work environment but also bolsters teamwork.

Strive for Professional Development

Investing in your employees' professional development is a win-win situation. Not only does it enhance their skills and productivity, but it also demonstrates that you value them and envision a future for them within the company. This investment can be on-the-job training, workshops, and seminars. These can ensure leaders that their teams stay updated with the latest industry trends, technologies, and best practices.

Chobani's Success in Effective Management

An example of a Limited Liability Company *(LLC)* that exemplifies effective management and leadership strategies is Chobani, a leading yogurt company in the U.S.

Chobani was founded by Hamdi Ulukaya in 2005. From the beginning, Ulukaya placed a significant emphasis on open communication. He often spends time on the factory floor, chatting with his employees, understanding their perspectives, and addressing their concerns. This approach has not only helped him earn the respect of his employees but has also fostered an environment of trust and transparency.

Regarding employee empowerment, Chobani has made headlines for its inclusive approach. In 2016, Ulukaya announced that he was giving all of his 2,000 full-time workers shares worth up to 10% of the company if it goes public or is sold, further fostering a sense of ownership and loyalty among his workforce.

As for recognition, Chobani goes beyond just providing competitive wages and full benefits. The company recognizes and celebrates the diverse backgrounds of its employees. Likewise, it received recognition for hiring refugees and providing them with opportunities to build a new life.

Regarding professional development, Chobani invests in its employees through its Chobani Scholarship program. This initiative offers a variety of courses in multiple languages to enhance their skills and capabilities.

Chapter 5
The Basics of LLC Taxation

Under certain conditions, an LLC can be taxed like a *C-corporation or an S-corporation*, making its tax situation more complex. Understanding LLC's taxation means knowing the tax rules, the impact of different business decisions on taxes, and how federal and state tax laws interact.

The Taxation Process

At the heart of LLC taxation lies the concept of *'pass-through'* taxation, discussed in the earlier chapters. In this system, the Internal Revenue Service *(IRS)* views the LLC as not a separate tax entity but an extension of its owners. Profits and losses' pass through' the LLC directly to its members. This contrasts with corporations, where profits are taxed at the corporate level.

The IRS classifies a one-owner LLC as a sole proprietorship and a multi-owner LLC as a partnership for taxation purposes. Consequently, the LLC must submit a **Partnership Return or Form 1065**, which documents the company's income, deductions, credits, and other tax-related details. Each member also gets a **Schedule K-1**, outlining their share of profits and losses.

As an LLC member, your income must be declared on your tax return, regardless of having received a distribution or not. Hence, you will be held accountable for tax on your share of the profits, even if the money has not hit your bank account. Such a situation might arise when the LLC retains earnings to pay for expenses or invest in the growth of the business.

Besides that, the IRS considers LLC members as self-employed for tax purposes. As a result, they are obliged to pay self-employment taxes, comprising both Social Security and Medicare taxes. These are determined based on the LLC's net earnings from self-employment and typically include its net profit. In contrast, corporate employees only cover half of these taxes, while the corporation handles the rest.

The pass-through taxation system offers several advantages but applies at the federal level. As such, consider additional taxes at the state and local levels. Some states, for instance, impose franchise taxes on LLCs, which can vary significantly depending on where your business operates.

Corporate Taxation

A flexible feature LLCs have is the option to elect corporate taxation. If the self-employment taxes are burdensome, they can be taxed as either a C-Corporation or an S-Corporation.

S Corporation Taxation

S Corporations are characterized as pass-through entities for tax purposes, much like the default taxation for LLCs. The corporation's income, losses, deductions, and credits flow to shareholders. A notable distinction is that S Corporation owners can permit some of their business profits to pass as earnings, while the remaining profits can be classified as dividends. These dividends are free from self-employment tax.

Why does that matter? As an employee, you only pay half of the Social Security and Medicare taxes. Then, your employer pays the other half. Hence, if an LLC owner takes some of their money as a *"paycheck"* from the business, they only have to pay half of the Social Security and Medicare taxes on that amount— 6.2% and 1.45%, respectively. The company pays the other half.

But what about the rest of the money? The leftover profits or *"dividends"* do not have to pay taxes on these. So, by taxing your LLC like an S Corporation, a business owner can save a lot of money in taxes.

Restrictions

S Corporations operate under certain constraints and prerequisites. For example, it can only have one class of stock. This single class of stock can have voting and nonvoting variations. Yet, all shares must have an identical claim on the corporation's earnings and assets. This limitation keeps the ownership structure of an S Corporation straightforward and unambiguous.

Furthermore, an S Corporation is capped at 100 shareholders. These shareholders can be individuals, certain trusts, or estates. However, they cannot be partnerships, corporations, or non-resident aliens. The limitation on the number and type of shareholders is designed to keep S Corporations closely held, meaning ownership is restricted to a relatively small group of people.

These restrictions are among the primary reasons certain businesses choose to be taxed as S Corporations. They provide a structure allowing businesses to benefit from pass-through taxation while maintaining a traditional corporate structure.

However, these may also present challenges. For example, an S Corporation may face difficulties raising capital since it cannot issue preferred stock, which might appeal more to investors. Similarly, the limitation on the number of shareholders can limit the company's growth potential and its ability to attract diverse investments.

C Corporation Taxation

When an LLC elects to be treated as a C Corporation for tax purposes, it becomes subject to double taxation. The LLC's income is taxed at the corporate level using the corporate tax rate. Then any dividends distributed to the members are taxed again on their tax returns.

While this can be seen as a disadvantage, C Corporation taxation can be beneficial in some scenarios. For instance, C Corporations can retain and reinvest earnings in the business at a lower corporate tax rate, which benefits companies planning to reinvest profits back into the business for expansion or other purposes.

Additionally, C Corporations can deduct the cost of fringe benefits provided to employees. If an LLC considers offering employee benefits, electing C Corporation taxation could present some tax advantages.

Federal, State, and Local Tax Obligations

The interplay between federal and state taxation is a critical factor in managing the financial situation of an LLC. While federal tax laws apply uniformly across the United States, state tax laws vary significantly.

Most states conform to the federal tax treatment, recognizing the pass-through nature of LLCs, where business income and losses are reported on the owner's tax returns. However, some states impose additional taxes or fees on businesses.

A prominent case is California, which enforces a franchise tax on LLCs. Essentially, this is a fee for conducting business as an LLC within the state. The starting franchise tax in California is $800, and it could escalate depending on the income of the LLC. This franchise tax remains mandatory, regardless of whether the LLC earns any income or remains inactive.

States like Texas and Illinois enforce a similar franchise tax or comparable fee, although their calculation methods and rates diverge from California's. For instance, Texas calculates its franchise tax depending on the LLC's margin, a number that can be established in various ways. Conversely, New York mandates a filing fee proportional to the LLC's income.

Certain states also necessitate that LLCs submit an annual or biennial report. This report typically comprises information about the LLC's business operations and its members. A filing fee usually accompanies this report.

Furthermore, multi-state operations introduce another layer of complexity. If an LLC does business in multiple states, it can be subject to taxes in all those states. The definition of *"doing business"* can vary from state to state. In some cases, it can trigger the need for foreign qualification, a process by which an LLC registers to do business in a state other than where it was formed.

Tax Advantages and Disadvantages of an LLC

To provide you with a comprehensive recap, here are the benefits of LLC regarding taxation, considering it is not taxed as a C corporation. However, not everything is perfect; it also has disadvantages and pitfalls.

Benefits of LLC Taxation

This section provides a brief overview of these benefits of LLC taxation, such as:

- **Flexible Tax Classification.** The IRS allows an LLC to be taxed as a sole proprietorship, partnership, S corporation, or C corporation. Each tax classification has its advantages and can be chosen based on the specific circumstances of your LLC.
- **Pass-Through Taxation.** Profits and losses are passed directly to the members of the LLC, which can help avoid the double taxation issue that corporations face.

- **Business Expenses Deduction.** LLC members can deduct legitimate business expenses. For instance, it includes costs related to running the business, such as rent, utilities, office supplies, business travel, and even certain meals.

Potential Pitfalls of LLC Taxation

Below are the potential pitfalls of taxation.

- **Self-Employment Taxes.** Profits distributed to LLC members are typically subject to self-employment taxes. These taxes go toward Social Security and Medicare and can be significant.
- **Potential for Higher Personal Taxes.** As profits pass through to members and are taxed at individual income tax rates, LLC owners could face higher taxes if their income tax rate is higher than the corporate tax rate.
- **Limited Fringe Benefits.** In contrast to corporations, owners of LLCs who are active in the business cannot deduct fringe benefits like health insurance and retirement plans.

Strategies for Maximizing LLC's Tax Advantages

When you employ strategic tax planning, an LLC can enhance its profitability, improve cash flow, and ultimately fuel its growth and success. The following section outlines several strategies for maximizing tax advantages in the context of an LLC.

Choose the Right Tax Classification

LLCs offer a unique level of flexibility when it comes to tax classification. They can be taxed as a sole proprietorship, a partnership, an S Corporation, or a C Corporation. Each classification carries different tax implications. For example, single-member LLCs are taxed as sole proprietorships and multi-member LLCs are taxed as partnerships, meaning the profits and losses are reported on the owner's tax returns. But as discussed earlier, they also have the option to be taxed as S Corporations or C Corporations.

For instance, if the members of an LLC are earning significantly more from the LLC than what would be considered a reasonable salary for the work they do, electing S Corporation status could save on self-employment taxes.

On the other hand, if an LLC plans to reinvest a substantial amount of its profits back into the business, choosing to be taxed as a C Corporation could be beneficial. Profits reinvested in the business might be subject to a lower corporate tax rate instead of the personal income tax rate of the owners.

Deduct Business Expenses

Running a business can come with many costs. *But did you know many of these can be deducted from your LLC's taxable income?* The IRS has a couple of rules, though. To count as a deduction, the expense must be ordinary and necessary. Examples of things you can deduct are your office rent, utilities, business travel, meals, supplies, equipment, and even business insurance premiums.

Suppose your LLC has an office, and you pay $20,000 yearly for it. That is a deductible expense, and it lowers your LLC's taxable income by $20,000. So, if you make $100,000 a year, you would only be taxed $80,000. For that reason, LLCs need to have a system to track and document all these expenses. That way, you will make the most of these deductions.

Employ Family Members

Hiring your family can help you save on taxes. Imagine being part of an LLC and in the 24% tax bracket. Suppose you get your 16-year-old kid to work for your business; this is what we call *"income shifting."* From its name, it is like moving money from a high-tax-rate group *(you)* to a lower-tax-rate group *(your child)*. In this scenario, the tax on the $12,000 salary you give to your child will be much less than if it were taxed at your rate.

Considering the payroll taxes, these are the taxes that an LLC needs to pay on wages to its workers, including family. However, if your LLC is taxed as a sole proprietorship or a partnership and each partner is a parent of the child, there is no need to pay Social Security and Medicare taxes on the wages you pay to your kid.

Remember, though, there are rules when hiring family, especially kids. Their work needs to be real, and their pay should match their work loads. Likewise, you must fill out all the right tax forms. Lastly, you must always follow state laws on child labor.

Contribute to a Retirement Plan

When a member contributes to a qualified retirement plan, those contributions are often tax-deductible, which reduces the member's taxable income. Examples of such plans include the *Simplified Employee Pension (SEP), Individual Retirement Accounts (IRA), Savings Incentive Match Plan for Employees (SIMPLE) IRA, and individual 401(k) plans*.

Consider the Simplified Employee Pension *(SEP)* IRA as an example. This plan lets you save a good chunk of your earnings with a limit of up to 25% of your income or a certain dollar amount, whichever is less. So, if you are an LLC member earning $100,000 and you put $10,000 into a SEP IRA, you only need to pay tax on $90,000 that year. Depending on your tax bracket, that could mean big savings.

However, the money you put into these plans is locked in until you retire and taking it out early can mean penalties. So, if you need the cash soon, it might be better to hold off on these plans, even if they could lower your taxes. That said, these accounts can be a great way to build up your nest egg for the future. Just remember, rules and who can join these retirement plans can change a lot and may differ from one plan to the next.

Take Advantage of Tax Credits

Tax credits are not the same as deductions; they directly reduce the tax amount that an LLC must pay. For instance, after all your earnings and deductions, you owe $10,000 in taxes but have a tax credit of $3,000, which means you get to deduct the $3,000 directly from your tax amount. Hence, you will only pay $7,000 instead of $10,000.

However, it is different from a tax deduction. A tax deduction lowers your taxable income based on your top federal income tax bracket's percentage. If you have a tax deduction of $3,000, and your tax bracket is 24%, this will only reduce your tax bill by $320 *(24% of $3,000)* rather than the full $3,000. This makes tax credits more valuable than deductions since they offer bigger savings.

There are several tax credits made explicitly for businesses, including LLCs. Here are a few examples:

- **Small Business Health Care Tax Credit.** This tax credit is available to businesses that provide health insurance to their employees. The IRS offers this to encourage smaller businesses to provide health insurance benefits.
- **Work Opportunity Tax Credit.** This tax credit is designed to encourage businesses to hire individuals from certain groups who have consistently faced significant barriers to employment.
- **Research & Experimentation Tax Credit.** Often referred to as the R&D Tax Credit, this is available to businesses that incur expenses for performing qualified research activities.

Hiring a Tax Professional

Even though tax-saving strategies exist, they can still be complex, and the best strategies often depend on an LLC's unique circumstances. Therefore, consider consulting with a tax professional to ensure you fully understand your tax obligations and opportunities.

Reasons to Hire a Tax Professional

Dealing with taxes for your LLC can be challenging, and mistakes can be expensive and lead to missing out on possible savings. To avoid this, consider hiring a tax advisor, and here is why:

Offer In-Depth Knowledge and Expertise

Tax laws are constantly shifting and can be rather complex. This is where a tax professional can assist. They are like a seasoned pilot steering through stormy weather, aiding your business in adapting to evolving tax laws. Likewise, they will ensure that your business adheres to the latest regulations and benefits from any possible tax advantages.

For instance, if a new law increases deductions for some business expenses, your tax professional will alert and show you how to leverage it. This proactive approach ensures that your LLC remains compliant while maximizing potential tax savings.

Save Time

Time, as they say, is money. The taxing task of figuring out taxes, comprehending deductions, and filling out forms can consume hours you could utilize to grow your business. Hiring a tax professional is akin to gaining extra hours in your day. They will manage the accumulated tax paperwork, freeing you to concentrate on building your business. Imagine the relief of knowing that someone else is sorting out the tax specifics while you focus on expanding, developing new products, or enhancing customer relationships.

Avoid Mistakes

When taxes are not filed accurately, it can be like stepping on a landmine. As such, one wrong step can result in penalties or an IRS audit. Evading these potential financial and legal complications makes it crucial to file your taxes correctly. This is where a tax professional becomes your safety net. They will ensure everything on your tax forms is accurate, helping you avoid costly mistakes.

Duties of a Tax Professional

Tax professionals serve as more than just number crunchers; they can become crucial allies in the success story of a Limited Liability Company (LLC). Their areas of expertise are wide-ranging, facilitating the smooth operation of your business in alignment with tax laws. Below are some of the responsibilities you can anticipate them to undertake.

Tax Preparation

Preparing and submitting tax returns can appear overwhelming, especially for LLCs, where taxation can be more intricate. A tax professional, equipped with a thorough understanding of current tax laws, assumes this responsibility. They prepare your LLC's tax returns with the highest degree of accuracy, ensuring each line complies with federal and state regulations. For instance, if your LLC has opted to be taxed as an S Corporation, the tax professional would prepare Form 1120S and the necessary Schedule K-1s for the members of the LLC.

Tax Planning

Beyond the annual submission of taxes, tax professionals also extend their expertise to strategic tax planning. They do not only focus on the current tax season but plan several steps, like a grandmaster in chess, considering how every decision today could impact your tax scenario tomorrow. Whether there is a potential business expansion, a new investment, or alterations in the company structure, your tax professional evaluates the tax implications of each scenario. They function as your strategic partner, ensuring your tax position is optimized for the current year and many years ahead. Their advice can influence critical decisions, from your business structure to managing expenses and income, aiming to maximize tax savings.

Audit Support

Facing an audit from the Internal Revenue Service (IRS) can be a nerve-wracking experience. However, the presence of a tax professional can make it less intimidating. They can steer you through the audit process, offering expert representation and advocating. For instance, if the IRS questions deductions claimed on your LLC's tax return, the tax professional could provide documentation that supports those deductions and explain why they are allowable under the tax code.

Tax Forms

To give you an overview, here are some common tax forms you may need for your LLC, depending on how it is taxed and other business specifics.

- **Form 1040 (U.S. Individual Income Tax Return).** Used to file annual income taxes. Additionally, suppose your LLC is single-membered and treated as a disregarded entity for tax purposes. In that case, the income or loss of the LLC is reported on Schedule C of your Form 1040.

- **Form 1065.** Relevant for LLC consisting of multiple members and is taxed as a partnership. It lets you document your business operations' income, gains, deductions, losses, and credits. Additionally, each member must complete the Schedule K-1 section of the form that records their share of the LLC's profits or losses.
- **Form 1120S.** For those LLCs that choose to be taxed as an S Corporation, you would file Form 1120S, the U.S. Income Tax Return for an S Corporation. Like Form 1065, this form reports income, losses, and dividends.
- **Form 8832 and Form 2553.** These are Entity Classification Election and Election by a Small Business Corporation forms, respectively. If you wish to change your LLC's tax status to a corporation or S Corporation, you will use these forms.
- **Form 940 and Form 941.** If you hired employees, then you will need to report employment taxes using these forms. Form 940 is used to report federal unemployment taxes. Likewise, it is used to report withholdings for Medicare, Social Security, and federal income tax.
- **Form 1099-NEC.** This form is used by businesses to report payments of $600 or more to nonemployees, such as independent contractors. Essentially, it is for reporting income, not part of the regular wages, salaries, or tips.

Remember, this is not an exhaustive list; other forms may be necessary depending on your circumstances. As always, consulting with a tax professional is highly recommended to ensure you are filing all the required forms correctly.

Exercise: Determining your LLC's Taxation

This exercise is designed to help you apply the concepts from this chapter to your own business situation.

- **Understand Your Tax Structure.** What type of taxation structure does your LLC currently use (partnership, S Corporation, or C Corporation), and why was this choice made?
- **Analyzing Your Tax Deductions.** List five business expenses that you currently claim as tax deductions. Are there any other expenses you can deduct that you are not claiming?
- **Planning for State Taxes.** In which state(s) does your LLC operate? Research and summarize the state tax obligations for an LLC in those states.
- **Maximize Tax Advantages.** From the strategies discussed in the chapter, choose one that you are not currently employing. How could this strategy benefit your business?
- **Role of a Tax Professional.** If you already have a tax professional, discuss a situation where they have provided significant value to your LLC. However, if you do not have a tax professional, outline a situation where you believe a tax professional could have helped your business navigate a challenging tax situation.

IRS treats LLCs as "pass-through" entities, causing members to report income on personal tax returns and pay Social Security and Medicare taxes. LLCs can elect S-Corporation or C Corporation tax models, with the potential for significant tax savings or reinvestment benefits but also risks like restrictions or double taxation. With federal, state, and local taxes, LLCs face various implications, like business expense deductions, self-employment taxes, and higher personal taxes. Given LLC taxation's complexity, a tax professional's assistance is recommended to handle tax laws and documentation, offer strategic planning and audit support, ensure regulatory compliance, and enable business growth.

Chapter 6

Legal Considerations for Your LLC

Understanding the legal landscape of your LLC is an ongoing process requiring constant attention and vigilance, not just a mere item on your task list. The dynamic regulations shaping the business world are complex, changing with societal progress and new legislative precedents. Comprehension of these can be the difference between success and potentially serious repercussions.

This chapter will cover numerous key aspects of LLC operations, including protecting personal assets and handling legal disputes. As well as the impact of intellectual property rights on your LLC, a business aspect gaining importance in the digital age.

Personal Liability Protection

As previously discussed in the first chapter, personal liability protection is one of the most distinctive characteristics of a Limited Liability Company. Below is a brief review of the aspects of personal liability protection.

- **Asset Protection.** Members' assets, such as homes or savings, are protected from claims and legal judgments resulting from the LLC's operations. In short,

members are not held personally accountable for business debts. Thus, creditors cannot pursue personal assets to pay these off.
- **Separate Legal Entity.** The LLC is seen as a separate legal entity, which means it has its rights and responsibilities separate from its owners. This separation enables it to own assets, enter into contracts, sue or be sued in its name, and be held accountable for its actions and liabilities without directly implicating the personal assets of its members.

Piercing the Corporate Veil

Personal liability protection provides a significant safety net for those who own businesses. Nonetheless, this protection is not absolute. Consider a hypothetical situation involving a boutique owner Sarah who opts to form a Limited Liability Company *(LLC)* for her business.

The LLC that Sarah establishes, known as *"Boutique Bliss,"* allows her to benefit from personal liability protection. Sarah would not be personally liable for these business debts if the company were to go bankrupt or face a significant financial lawsuit. The safety net in this context is evident: *the financial aspects of Sarah's personal life are separate from her business.*

Now let us suppose Sarah starts to use the funds of the LLC for personal expenses, such as going on vacation or buying groceries, causing the boundaries between her personal and business finances to blur. From a legal standpoint, Sarah ignores the separation between herself and the LLC. In such instances, if a lawsuit occurs or the business goes bankrupt, the court could decide that Sarah and Boutique Bliss are not separate entities. This is often referred to as *'piercing the corporate veil.'*

To further explain, this legal doctrine allows courts to disregard the limited liability protection typically afforded to business owners. Under specific circumstances, courts may ignore the legal separation between a business entity, like an LLC, and its owners, making the owners personally liable for the company's debts or legal responsibilities. This act of piercing the corporate veil is usually done when certain actions or behaviors undermine the distinctness of the business entity, treating it as an alter ego or extension of the owners.

Returning to our example, Sarah's protection from personal liability could be revoked, and her assets may be at risk. By intertwining her business and personal affairs, she pierces the corporate veil and could face penalties.

Maintaining Your LLC's Protection

Setting up and providing the financial means for your Limited Liability Company *(LLC)* signifies the start of your entrepreneurial journey. However, preserving its integrity, including its separate status from your dealings, is a continuous endeavor. Remember that your LLC is not just a legal framework; it functions as your business ally.

Suppose you handle it with the requisite diligence, respect, and attention it deserves. In that case, it will reciprocate by offering you the protection, credibility, and growth potential of a successful LLC's defining features. Sticking to the procedures outlined below will ensure that your LLC remains a strong and autonomous entity, safeguarding your wealth from business debts and creating the path for long-term business expansion.

Maintain a Clear Distinction Between Personal and Business Matters

The integrity of your Limited Liability Company (LLC) rests on the firm separation between your personal and business activities. This distinction must be upheld regardless of the size or structure of your LLC. Here are several strategies to ensure your business remains an independent entity.

Establish Separate Bank Accounts

Let us revisit Sarah and Boutique Bliss. Sarah's severe error was utilizing her LLC's bank account to support her activities, thus compromising the corporate veil. A clear separation of personal and business bank accounts is crucial to prevent this. As such, your LLC's account must never be used for personal expenses, irrespective of how small they might seem. The reverse is also true; personal funds should not be used for business purposes. Combining the two can obscure the boundaries between personal and business matters. A useful strategy is to regard your LLC as separate from yourself. Execute all transactions, buying office supplies or investing in business growth, under the LLC's name.

Conduct Agreements in the LLC's Name

Ensure all contracts, agreements, and financial transactions are completed under your LLC's name. This applies to emails, letters, or any written business-related communication. While it may seem monotonous to sign each email or contract as *'John Doe, member of JD LLC'* rather than simply *'John Doe,'* these small habits reinforce the separate status of your LLC. For instance, if you are signing a lease agreement for your business office space, ensure the contract is between the landlord and your LLC, not you as an individual.

Maintain Adequate Funding

An LLC with sufficient funding is less likely to be seen as an extension of your finances. This point relates to our earlier conversation about financing options. Whatever method you choose should provide enough capital to establish the LLC and cover operational costs and potential liabilities.

Insufficient or inconsistent funding can result in a situation called *'undercapitalization.'* Courts often consider this when determining whether the corporate veil was compromised. For example, if your LLC consistently struggles to meet its financial obligations due to a lack of funds, it might be seen as merely an *'extension'* of your finances. This could put your assets at risk, as they might be used to pay the LLC's debts and liabilities.

Keep Comprehensive and Consistent Records

Proper record-keeping is concrete proof of separating your personal and business operations. Keep clear and formal records of all business transactions, decisions, and meetings. If you are the sole member of your LLC, you may think, *'Why do I need formal meeting minutes? I am only meeting with myself.'* Remember, the objective is to document your decisions as business actions, not personal ones. Ensuring all your decisions are supported by well-documented minutes helps maintain your LLC's status as a separate entity.

Fulfill Legal Obligations

Meeting all your legal obligations as an LLC is compulsory. Failure to meet these responsibilities can result in fines, penalties, or even the dissolution of your LLC. This includes the timely payment of taxes, renewal of licenses, and compliance with state-specific reporting requirements.

Maintain a Legitimate Business Purpose

An LLC's distinct status is maintained by having a genuine business purpose. This is typically outlined in the articles of organization and should comprehensively reflect the business activities your company plans to undertake. Likewise, it serves as a reminder that the business should primarily focus on activities that align with its stated objective. Deviating significantly from the stated purpose will compromise the corporate veil. Hence, it could suggest to courts that your LLC was formed under pretenses or is merely a shell for personal liability evasion.

Legal Disputes and Lawsuits

Though legal disputes and lawsuits pertain to conflicts, they are not entirely the same. Legal disputes refer to disagreements that may be resolved through negotiation, mediation, or other alternative dispute resolution mechanisms. On the other hand, lawsuits refer to formal legal actions brought before a court to resolve these disputes when other methods fail or are inappropriate. While undesirable, both are often an unavoidable reality for businesses. These legal conflicts can stem from various sources and happen at any point in a business's lifecycle.

Types of Legal Disputes Involving LLCs

Despite the many benefits of LLCs, members often find themselves amid legal conflicts. If not resolved swiftly and amicably, such disagreements can destabilize the business and hinder its progress. Here are some of the most common legal disputes you can take note of this so that you are aware of what to do when faced with this challenge. Note that the origins and nature of these disputes vary, each calling for different legal tactics and strategies to prevent escalation of the dispute into a lawsuit.

Internal Disputes

Internal disputes refer to conflicts that take place within the Limited Liability Company (LLC) itself. These conflicts often arise among the members or between the members and managers. The origin of such disputes could be disagreements over the distribution of profits, allocation of management responsibilities, or potential violations of the operating agreement.

Let us delve into this topic with an example for better understanding. Imagine an LLC with three members: Alice, Bob, and Charles. They all agreed upon an operating agreement that stated profits would be shared equally among them. However, trouble starts when Bob, who has contributed a higher initial capital to the LLC, argues for a larger share of the profits. If negotiations fail and a resolution is not reached, this disagreement could escalate into a lawsuit. This could cause substantial harm to the harmony and functioning of the LLC.

On the other hand, **fiduciary disputes** usually crop up when a member is perceived to have acted in their interest to the detriment of the company. In our example, if Bob decides to seize a business opportunity meant for the LLC for his benefit, he could be accused of breaching his fiduciary duty. This would result in mistrust among the members, leading to a lawsuit. Disputes among LLC members also arise from differing interpretations of the operating agreement. This often happens if the operating agreement is not drafted clearly.

To prevent such disagreements, have a comprehensive and well-drafted operating agreement. This agreement should clearly outline the mechanisms for profit distribution, the roles and responsibilities of management, and the procedures for admitting new members or handling exits. Regular communication among members and managers can also help prevent misunderstandings.

Workplace Disputes

Imagine a scenario where David Lochridge, who OceanGate once employed, initiates a lawsuit against the firm for improper dismissal. He contends that his termination resulted from his expressed worries about the safety of the company's underwater vehicle, the Titan. Lochridge's duties as a submarine pilot and underwater inspector were to secure the well-being of all crew members and clients during underwater and surface activities.

Instead of responding to his worries, OceanGate let Lochridge go, allotting him just around ten minutes to pack up his belongings and vacate the premises. Reacting to his sudden dismissal, he brought a lawsuit against the firm, claiming wrongful termination. He posited that his dismissal was a retaliatory measure because he expressed concerns about the safety of the Titan submersible. A disagreement of this kind would require a comprehensive investigation into the practices of the company and the conditions surrounding Lochridge's dismissal.

Workplace disputes like these in Limited Liability Companies can be intricate and challenging, typically needing intervention and mediation from external legal entities or extensive internal investigations. These disputes are usually accusations of unfair dismissal, discrimination, and wage and hour violations.

Implementing a strong human resources policy, fair employment practices, and maintaining a secure, inclusive work atmosphere can help avoid such disagreements. Employment contracts should be explicit about the employment terms, and any dismissals should adhere to legal and ethical guidelines. Regular training to employees and management about workplace rights, discrimination, and harassment can also play a crucial role in maintaining a harmonious work environment.

Handling Lawsuits and Disputes

Addressing lawsuits and disputes can be tiring as it demands a profound comprehension of legal intricacies, strategic foresight, and, not least, immense patience. This section provides general guidelines and tips that you could do when confronting such trials.

Adopting a Proactive Approach

Taking a proactive approach means foreseeing possible problems and putting solutions in place before they occur rather than simply responding to events as they happen. This demands foresight, meticulous planning, and a thorough grasp of all relevant laws and regulations. Within a legal context, a proactive approach could stop small misunderstandings from growing into major disputes or lawsuits. Therefore, safeguarding a company's resources, reputation, and relationships.

This strategy involves creating comprehensive operating agreements that clearly define roles, responsibilities, and procedures, thus reducing potential stakeholder misunderstandings. Equitable policies could also be set up in recruitment, compensation, promotions, and terminations. Due to these measures, compliance with employment laws is ensured, and a positive working environment is fostered. As such, employees who believe they are treated fairly are less likely to take legal action against their employer.

Consider a previous example involving Acme LLC and Zenith Corp. If Acme had adopted a more proactive approach and conducted a thorough patent search before developing their innovative drug. They might have discovered Zenith Corp's existing patent. This information could have allowed them to either negotiate a licensing agreement with Zenith Corp or alter their drug to avoid patent infringement, perhaps warding off the looming lawsuit entirely.

Seeking Legal Guidance

When conflict arises within an LLC, one of the most crucial first steps is to secure proficient legal guidance. An experienced lawyer's role transcends the simple provision of legal advice; they offer strategic direction in navigating the complex maze of legal matters, represent the company's best interests during negotiations, and vigorously defend the company in court should the dispute escalate to full-fledged litigation.

Think of Legal counsel as a lighthouse in a storm, illuminating the path through choppy, uncertain waters. Their expertise helps to interpret complex legal documents and regulations, assess the strength of a claim, and advise on the appropriate course of action. They can also facilitate or participate in dispute resolution processes such as negotiation, mediation, or arbitration, providing an invaluable perspective and seeking the best possible outcome for their client.

Moreover, they can help an LLC understand the potential consequences of a dispute, both immediate and long-term. This insight can be invaluable in making informed decisions, especially when balancing the desire for an immediate resolution with potential future implications.

To revisit the hypothetical dispute between Alice, Bob, and Charles, a skilled attorney can interpret the operating agreement, clarify its implications for each party, and propose viable options for resolution. They could evaluate the strength of each member's position, guide the negotiation process, and suggest compromises that could help avoid litigation.

The attorney would become an even more critical ally if the disagreement escalated into a courtroom battle. They would represent the members in court, articulating their cases and defending their rights. This representation provides a measure of protection against potential legal ramifications, as well as ensures that the members' interests are vigorously pursued. Legal counsel plays a crucial role in the dispute resolution process by providing both a shield and a sword.

Having Effective Negotiation and Mediation

Frequently, the escalation of disputes can be preemptively countered via non-confrontational strategies such as negotiation or mediation. These methods provide avenues to reach mutually satisfactory resolutions without taking up the dispute in the courtroom.

Negotiation is a direct dialogue between conflicting parties to resolve their dispute amicably. Here, parties attempt to communicate their issues, needs, and interests, striving to find a middle ground. The strength of negotiation lies in its flexibility and control, as parties can directly influence the outcome and tailor it to their unique circumstances. Moreover, this process is usually quicker and less expensive than litigation, reducing the financial strain often associated with legal disputes.

Mediation, on the other hand, involves the intervention of a neutral third party or mediator. The mediator does not impose a resolution but facilitates the conversation between the disputing parties, helping them to uncover mutually beneficial solutions. Mediation can be particularly beneficial when the relationship between the parties needs to be preserved, as it promotes understanding and collaboration rather than antagonism.

Negotiation and mediation are more cost-effective and expedient than litigation. They also maintain a level of privacy that's absent in the public realm of a courtroom, thereby helping to protect the reputation of the involved parties. Furthermore, these methods reduce hostility, often transforming a potential zero-sum situation into an opportunity for mutual gains. This preservation of relationships can be crucial in business contexts, where ongoing collaboration might still be necessary post-dispute.

Should the opposing parties successfully reach an agreement through these non-aggressive means, they can avoid the hefty financial toll and potential reputation damage that comes with litigation. Nonetheless, these techniques hinge on collaboration and willingness from all parties to find a resolution. More formal dispute resolution methods, such as arbitration or litigation, may be required without this cooperative spirit.

Leveraging Alternative Dispute Resolution (ADR) Methods

When traditional negotiation or mediation procedures fail to reconcile differences and the involved parties wish to steer clear of courtroom proceedings, Alternative Dispute Resolution *(ADR)* methods, such as arbitration, offer a viable alternative.

Arbitration is an ADR technique wherein a neutral third party or panel, called an arbitrator or arbitration panel, listens to the arguments from both sides, reviews evidence, and then makes a decision. Unlike a mediator, an arbitrator has the authority to decide the dispute. The role of the arbitrator is akin to that of a judge, and they are typically an expert in the field related to the dispute. The proceedings are more informal than court trials, and the rules of evidence are more relaxed. These conditions often result in a more expedited and less expensive process than traditional litigation.

The arbitrator will listen to each party's case, review the evidence provided, and decide. Depending on the agreement between the parties, the decision or the *'award'* can be binding or non-binding. A binding decision is final and enforceable by law, similar to a court judgment. Contrarily, a non-binding decision serves more as a recommendation, and parties can pursue a trial if dissatisfied with the outcome.

Another crucial aspect of arbitration is that it is usually *confidential*. This feature can be precious for businesses, as it allows them to manage disputes without attracting public scrutiny or damaging their reputation. Nevertheless, arbitration may not be the best fit for every dispute. Yet, it is most effective when the parties have a relatively equal power dynamic and are willing to accept the arbitrator's decision.

In cases with a significant power imbalance or when a party wants the ability to appeal, court proceedings might still be the best option. Arbitration remains a compelling alternative to courtroom battles, offering faster, cost-effective, and private means to resolve disputes.

Contracts and Agreements

Contracts are the lifeblood of business relationships. These legal documents, binding and enforceable by law, serve as the foundation on which businesses build and foster relationships with various stakeholders such as clients, vendors, partners, and employees. A contract stipulates each party's responsibilities, rights, and obligations, offering a safety net against potential misunderstandings or disagreements that could otherwise lead to legal disputes.

Imagine an orchestra without a conductor; every musician performing independently without synchronization would result in chaos rather than harmony. Similarly, business without contracts would lead to confusion and misunderstandings, often resulting in legal disputes and even lawsuits. The role of a contract in business is much like an orchestra conductor, providing direction, setting the tempo, and ensuring all parties work in harmony toward a shared goal.

For instance, consider a simple scenario of an LLC —*let us call it CreativeDesigns*— agreeing with a client to design a website. A detailed contract would outline the project's scope, timeline, the LLC's compensation, and the terms for addressing potential disagreements. The contract ensures that both CreativeDesigns and the client clearly understand what is expected, thereby reducing the risk of misunderstandings or disagreements.

However, it is not just about avoiding disputes. Contracts also play a vital role in protecting a company's interests and assets. Confidentiality agreements, for instance, help ensure that sensitive business information does not end up in the wrong hands. A well-drafted contract can also serve as a shield, protecting the company from potential legal liabilities.

Types of Contracts for LLCs

There are a variety of contracts that may be necessary depending on the nature and scope of your company. These agreements provide clarity, protect the interests of the business, and form the legal foundation for its interactions with various parties. Some types of contracts that are commonly used by LLCs include the following:

- **Operating Agreement.** As previously mentioned, the operating agreement plays a fundamental role within an LLC's structure. This pivotal document encapsulates key details about the company's governance, such as delineating member responsibilities, outlining the distribution methodology for profits and losses, and defining the procedures for changes in membership, including departures or transfers of ownership.
- **Service Agreement.** Also known as a **general service contract**, this agreement outlines the terms of service to be provided by the LLC. It includes details such as the scope of work, timelines, payment terms, and what happens if the contract is breached.
- **Employment Agreement.** An employment agreement becomes necessary if the LLC hires employees. This contract details the responsibilities of the employee, the compensation they will receive, the terms of their employment, and the conditions under which they can be terminated.

- **Non-Disclosure Agreement (NDA).** Such a contract is essential if the LLC deals with sensitive information. The NDA protects business secrets by preventing employees or other parties from disclosing confidential information.
- **Lease Agreement.** A lease agreement with the landlord will be required if the LLC operates from a rented office space. This contract specifies the terms and conditions of the lease, such as rent payment, duration of the lease, and maintenance responsibilities.
- **Vendor/Supplier Agreement.** These contracts set forth the terms and conditions under which the vendor or supplier will provide goods or services to the LLC. They cover delivery schedules, quality standards, and payment terms.
- **Partnership Agreement.** Suppose the LLC is joining a joint venture or partnership with another company. In that case, a partnership agreement will be necessary to define each party's roles, responsibilities, profit-sharing, and exit strategies.

Intellectual Property Rights

In our present society, propelled by knowledge and creativity, it is common to find that much of a business's worth lies in its intellectual property. Such properties allow companies to protect and yield profit from their inventive efforts. For instance, whether a business is seeking a patent for an innovative invention, registering a trademark for an appealing brand name, or establishing a copyright for a unique software program, it can secure exclusive rights to its intellectual property.

Yet, recognize that these entities are distinct. Establishing these rights blocks others from capitalizing on their creations without permission. Likewise, it offers a competitive advantage in the commercial arena. To illustrate this point further, consider the case study involving Snapchat and its legal tussle with Facebook, which underscores the importance of safeguarding intellectual property rights.

Snapchat and Its Ephemeral Messaging Feature

Initially released in 2011, Snapchat presented a unique and fresh concept in the developing social media scene: *ephemeral messaging, or messages that would automatically delete after a short period.* This innovative feature, which formed the core of Snapchat's value proposition, was its intellectual property and gave it a significant competitive advantage.

However, Snapchat's unique selling point did not go unnoticed. Other major players in the tech industry soon launched similar features on their platforms, noticeably Instagram with their *'stories'* feature and, later, Facebook. Both platforms were owned by the tech giant Facebook, Inc., now Meta Platforms, Inc.

This action ignited a significant dispute in the tech world. Snapchat, feeling threatened, may have sought to protect its intellectual property. However, the intricate nature of software patents and the general difficulty in patenting a user interface or a concept hindered Snapchat.

In the Snapchat case, the company could have pursued a patent for the unique algorithm that powered the ephemeral messaging feature, thereby legally protecting its intellectual property. However, one of the limitations of patents is that they do not extend to internet-based innovations. Thus, Snapchat has been unable to successfully sue Facebook for copying its unique feature.

Types of Intellectual Property

Understanding the fundamental differences between patents, copyrights, trademarks, and trade secrets will help you protect and leverage your innovative assets. Below are the distinguishing features of these four types of intellectual property.

Patents

Patents represent a powerful tool for protecting inventions. They give inventors the exclusive right to prevent others from making, using, or selling their inventions for a specific period, usually 20 years from the application date.

What sets patents apart is their application to specific inventions that meet the criteria of novelty, non-obviousness, and usefulness. The invention could range from a new process, machine, or composition of matter to any useful improvement of existing ones.

Take, for instance, Google's patent for their *'PageRank'* algorithm, which forms the basis of their search technology. This patent effectively prevents other companies from replicating Google's unique method of webpage ranking.

Copyrights

An example of copyright is J.K. Rowling's Harry Potter series. Unauthorized reproductions or adaptations of her books would infringe upon her copyrights.

Here you can see that while patents protect inventions, copyrights safeguard original works of authorship, including literary, dramatic, musical, and artistic creations, as well as computer software and architecture. Once an idea is expressed in a tangible form— *a novel penned, a song recorded, or a software coded*— it can be protected under copyright laws.

The beauty of copyright is in its automatic protection upon creating the work. Though registration offers additional benefits, it is not a requirement. Copyrights prevent unauthorized reproduction, distribution, public performance, or creation of derivative work.

Trademarks

Picture yourself stepping into a city filled with shops, none with distinct names or recognizable logos. *Identifying one shop from another would be arduous, would it not?* This situation illustrates the role of trademarks, which grant your business its unique *'identity.'* Trademarks may come in logos, symbols, names, or designs—essentially anything exclusive to your products or services and distinguishes them in the marketplace.

However, trademarks reside in their dual function. On one side, they establish and fortify your unique brand identity. On the flip side, they safeguard against potential consumer mix-ups, prohibiting others from capitalizing on your brand's reputation by offering similar products or services.

Take a moment to contemplate the emblematic *'Golden Arches'* of McDonald's. This iconic symbol is instantly identifiable and has been ingrained in the minds of consumers all over the world. The strength of their trademark empowers McDonald's to prevent any other restaurant from using a similar logo. Thereby circumventing potential customer confusion and preserving the brand's distinct identity.

Trade Secrets

While not as immediately noticeable as other types of intellectual property, trade secrets play an equally pivotal role. They safeguard information that is both confidential and integral to your business, giving you a competitive leg-up. Common examples include secret recipes, customer databases, and manufacturing techniques.

Unlike other forms of intellectual property, trade secrets do not have a defined term of protection. They remain protected as long as they remain confidential and provide a competitive advantage.

Exercise: Understanding of Legal Considerations

The following exercise has been meticulously designed to aid you in assessing your understanding of the chapter. Incorporated here is a variety of hypothetical situations that you might encounter while managing your own Limited Liability Company. There are thought-provoking questions woven into this exercise that are relevant to your potential future Limited Liability Company. Upon completing this exercise, you are encouraged to cross-reference your responses with the concepts elucidated in the chapter.

Part 1: Personal Liability Protection

1. Imagine being a member of a newly formed LLC called *"Innovative Designs LLC"* that designs and sells bespoke furniture. One of the pieces of furniture your company sold had a defect and caused injury to a customer. The customer decided to sue the company for damages.

    a. Explain how personal liability protection works for an LLC in this situation.
    b. What assets are protected, and what could be at risk?

Part 2: Legal Disputes and Lawsuits

1. Innovative Designs LLC is now facing a dispute with one of its suppliers over the quality of raw materials provided.

    a. What are the steps the company should take to address this dispute?
    b. Discuss how negotiation, mediation, or arbitration could resolve this dispute before it escalates to a lawsuit.
2. Write a brief scenario describing a potential legal dispute within an LLC. Outline the steps to resolve the dispute, including negotiation, mediation, or al-

ternative dispute resolution *(ADR)* as part of your solution.

Part 3: Contracts and Agreements

1. As a part of Innovative Designs LLC, you plan to hire a new employee and enter into an agreement with a new supplier.

    a. List and describe the contracts and agreements the LLC should consider in both cases.
    b. What are the crucial elements that these agreements should include?

2. Draft a simple confidentiality agreement between an LLC and a new employee with access to sensitive business information.

Part 4: Intellectual Property Rights

1. Innovative Designs LLC has designed a unique piece of furniture that has become very popular, and they want to protect their design.

    a. Discuss the different types of intellectual property protection available and suggest the most suitable one for this unique design.
    b. Explain the process the LLC would need to undergo to secure this protection.

2. Think about the possible LLC that you are planning to form and manage. What intellectual property assets might this LLC own? What steps would you take to protect these assets?

Thus, in an LLC, personal liability protection protects members' assets from business liabilities, treating the company separately. Courts could hold owners liable for company debts if personal and business finances merge. Clear financial separation, comprehensive operating agreements, and fair practices can prevent disputes. Expert legal advice is critical for conflict resolution and defense in potential lawsuits. Alternative dispute resolution methods offer quick and private solutions. Contracts clarify business relationships and responsibilities, reducing misunderstandings. Intellectual property rights protect unique business assets, providing a competitive edge.

Chapter 7
Maintaining Compliance

Beyond taxation, there are several other essential responsibilities that LLCs must fulfill to ensure smooth operations and ongoing compliance with regulatory standards. This segment will examine these key duties, including tax filing and regular reporting, renewing your LLC, and obtaining the necessary business licenses and permits.

Tax Filing

All businesses are required to file their taxes. Depending on the nature and location of your business, you may be required to file various tax documents at local, state, and federal levels. These could include income tax returns, sales tax returns, and payroll tax reports, to name a few.

Take, for example, a software development startup base in California. Apart from federal taxes, this firm would be mandated to submit California state taxes and, possibly, local taxes applicable to their city. If they employ a team, managing payroll taxes becomes another responsibility. Moreover, if their business involves the sale of tangible goods, they will need to handle sales tax.

Regardless of the size or the industry in which an LLC operates, paying taxes forms a significant part of its operational duties. Abiding by tax regulations is not merely a legal obligation; it is a factor influencing a business's standing, viability, and overall success.

Importance of Tax Filing

Paying taxes reflects an LLC's integrity, responsibility, and societal contribution. Some of the importance of tax filing for an LLC and how it impacts various facets of the business and its stakeholders are discussed below.

Fulfilling Legal Obligations

At the most fundamental level, paying taxes is a legal requirement for all businesses, including LLCs. The Internal Revenue Service *(IRS)* has established a comprehensive set of rules and guidelines for LLCs concerning their tax liabilities. This includes income taxes, self-employment taxes, and potentially, depending on the state, additional franchise or excise taxes. Non-compliance with these tax laws and failure to pay taxes in time can result in severe penalties, ranging from financial fines to criminal charges.

Financial Sustainability and Planning

Proper tax planning enables an LLC to account for this expense in its budget. This allows for better cash flow management, ensuring enough funds to cover taxes when they are due, and prevents the LLC from facing a cash crunch. Considering your tax liability will be beneficial since it can help you make decisions about investing in new projects, expanding the business, or reinvesting profits back into the company. Failure to do this can make you overestimate your available capital, leading to overinvestment and potential financial distress.

Social Responsibility and Reputation

Taxes are a primary source of revenue for the government, supporting public services such as education, infrastructure, and healthcare. By paying their fair share of taxes, LLCs contribute to the well-being of the communities they serve, which can enhance their reputation and standing.

In today's era of increased transparency and social consciousness, businesses are often scrutinized for their tax practices. Companies that fail to pay their taxes can face significant reputational damage, which can, in turn, affect customer trust and loyalty. In contrast, an LLC known for its ethical tax practices can use this as a point of differentiation, reinforcing its reputation as a responsible and trustworthy entity.

Investor Relations and Business Opportunities

For LLCs seeking investment or exploring business partnerships, a strong record of tax compliance can be a significant asset. Investors and potential business partners often undertake thorough due diligence before getting involved with an LLC. A history of timely and accurate tax payments will demonstrate your commitment to compliance and good financial management. It shows potential stakeholders that the business is reliable and reduces the perceived risk associated with the investment or partnership.

A Culture of Compliance

A successful LLC cultivates a culture of compliance, where tax obligations are seen not as a burden but as an integral aspect of the business's operations and strategy. This approach involves keeping updated with changing tax laws, using professional tax advice, and treating tax planning as an ongoing, proactive process.

Financial Reports

These documents provide an overview of an enterprise's fiscal health, detailing income, expenses, assets, and liabilities. Such information is essential for decision-making, planning, and securing investments or loans.

Consider a local family-owned restaurant, for instance. The owners need regular financial reports to monitor sales, track expenses, and measure profitability. A detailed monthly report reveals that high-end steak dishes are the most profitable items, while low-cost vegetarian dishes cost the business. This information could shape the future menu, pricing, and marketing strategies, illustrating the importance of financial reporting in everyday operations.

In larger corporations, these reports also play the same pivotal role. They are necessary for the board of directors to make informed strategic decisions. For instance, if a report highlights that a product line is underperforming, it might discontinue it and shift resources toward more profitable areas.

Contents of a Financial Report

Every financial report holds its significance and complexities, offering a thorough perspective of a company's financial well-being. While this information is essential, it can frequently be overwhelming. To make this more understandable, below are the contents of a financial report in detail, dissecting each component.

Balance Sheet

A balance sheet is a core part of a financial report, presenting a snapshot of a company's financial status at a particular moment. It enumerates the company's assets, liabilities, and shareholders' equity.

Consider a hypothetical company, TechGuru Ltd. Its balance sheet might display $2 million in assets, comprising cash, inventories, and property, among other items. The liabilities could amount to $1 million, including payables, loans, and other commitments. When liabilities are subtracted from assets, the remaining figure is the shareholders' equity, which would be $1 million.

Income Statement

An income statement, or *profit and loss statement,* offers a view of a company's profitability over a specific duration. It reports the company's revenues, costs, expenses, and net income or loss. Going back to TechGuru Ltd., if it generated $1 million in revenue but incurred $700 thousand in costs and expenses, the income statement would document a net income of $300 thousand, demonstrating profitability during that period.

Cash Flow Statement

A cash flow statement monitors the inflow and outflow of cash within a business, divided into operating, investing, and financing activities. For example, TechGuru's cash flow statement might indicate that it derived $500 thousand in cash from operating activities such as product sales, expended $200 thousand in investing activities like equipment purchases, and received three hundred thousand dollars from financing activities, such as loans or share issuance.

Statement of Changes in Equity

Should TechGuru issue new shares or disburse dividends, these transactions would be reflected in this statement, allowing stakeholders to monitor any alterations in ownership equity. The statement of changes in equity records shifts in the company's equity over a specific period. This report is crucial for understanding how a company's net worth fluctuates.

Notes to the Financial Statements

Notes play a role in understanding the specifics behind the figures reported in financial statements. They offer additional information about accounting policies, breakdowns of specific line items, and details about contingent liabilities or future commitments. For example, if TechGuru's balance sheet demonstrated a significant increase in property assets, they could include a note stating that the company has purchased a new office building, thereby explaining the substantial increase.

Independent Auditor's Report

Following the audit of TechGuru's financial statements, the auditor's report would assure shareholders and other stakeholders of the accuracy and reliability of the company's financial reporting. An independent auditor's report confirms the veracity and fairness of the financial statements. An external auditing firm typically prepares it and forms an integral part of the company's annual report.

Procedures for Tax Filing and Financial Reports

Fulfilling your reporting and tax filing obligations is essential, but it is not just about completing the documents. As such, understand too the deadlines and procedures for submission, which can vary significantly depending on the report or tax return in question.

Submission Deadlines

Financial reports generally have flexibility regarding when they are produced, as long as they are regularly generated for internal decision-making or as required by lenders or investors. However, tax filings are subject to strict deadlines the relevant tax authorities set.

For instance, in the United States, most businesses must file their income tax returns by April 15th or the next business day if that date falls on a weekend or holiday. Other types of taxes have different deadlines. Payroll taxes may need to be deposited semi-weekly or monthly, and sales tax returns may be due quarterly or annually.

Submission Procedures

The procedures for submitting these reports and filings can also vary. Many businesses nowadays use digital solutions, but check the rules and preferences of your particular jurisdiction or audience.

When submitting financial reports to a board of directors, for instance, an email or online portal might suffice. However, when filing taxes, follow the specific procedures outlined by your tax authority. While many services have moved online, some submissions may still require paper forms or physical presence.

Renewing Your LLC

When you start a limited liability company, it is not a *'set it and forget it'* type of arrangement. Like a garden, your LLC requires consistent maintenance to remain healthy and productive. One of the maintenance activities is the renewal process, which involves steps to keep your LLC active and in good standing.

Under this section is information about the penalties associated with neglecting LLC renewal. Hence, stay aware of your renewal deadlines and fulfill them diligently. After all, the success of your LLC depends not only on its profitability but also on its compliance with state obligations.

Penalties for Neglecting LLC Renewal

Failure to complete renewals, typically through annual reports or statements, in a timely manner can lead to severe consequences. Some of the potential penalties and implications that can arise from neglecting to renew your LLC include the following:

Monetary Penalties

The most immediate consequence of failing to renew your LLC on time is typically monetary. Each state has its own set of penalties for late renewal, usually as late fees. For instance, if you miss the deadline for filing an annual report in Florida, you will be charged a $400 late fee. This financial penalty is in addition to the standard filing fee.

Loss of Good Standing

Your LLC is in good standing when it meets all its obligations as specified by the state, such as filing annual reports and paying the necessary fees. Loss of good standing for an LLC can lead to severe consequences. Aside from facing penalties and fines, non-compliance can also result in the loss of potential business opportunities, as many entities prefer to deal with companies in good standing. Additionally, it may become more challenging to secure funding from investors or lenders who view the good standing status as an indication of a reliable, well-managed business.

Administrative Dissolution

If the late renewal of an LLC goes unaddressed for an extended period, the ultimate penalty is what's known as *'administrative dissolution.'* This term refers to the involuntary dissolution of an LLC by the state due to failure to comply with certain requirements, such as filing annual reports or paying fees.

Consequences of Dissolution

The dissolution of your Limited Liability Company (LLC) does not merely signify its end. It also triggers various significant repercussions. For starters, other businesses can utilize your LLC's name, potentially causing brand confusion or decreasing brand equity.

Additionally, the owners of the LLC may forfeit their limited liability protections. It implies that the owners could be held personally accountable if any business debts or liabilities were accumulated while the LLC was unsatisfactory. This situation would undermine one of the main advantages of creating an LLC, which is the protection of your assets.

Take, for example, a boutique clothing LLC in Washington State called *'Emerald Trends.'* If they neglect to renew their LLC and it undergoes administrative dissolution, the owners could be personally liable for any business debts. Should Emerald Trends owe money to suppliers or landlords, the owners could be sought after by those creditors for payment, risking their assets.

Reinstatement

Despite the occurrence of administrative dissolution, some states offer a pathway to regain good standing known as *'reinstatement.'* This process involves fulfilling the obligations that led to your LLC's dissolution, such as submitting overdue reports and paying unsettled fees. In addition to this, you will typically need to pay a reinstatement fee.

Referencing our previous example, *'Emerald Trends,'* they could request reinstatement to resurrect their dissolved LLC. To accomplish this, they would need to update all missed filings, settle any outstanding fees and penalties, and a reinstatement fee. However, reinstatement can be a complex and expensive procedure, making it far more favorable to prevent dissolution in the first place.

Understanding the Renewal Process

The LLC renewal process is a procedure that each LLC must go through to keep its status active. Generally, the process requires the company to provide up-to-date information about its operation; *It is how to inform the state about your business's status.*

The renewal process often involves filing a document—*commonly an annual report or similar*—with the state agency that handles business registrations, such as the Secretary of State's office.

The Process of Renewing an LLC

Renewing an LLC involves several steps, such as:

Verify Your State's Prerequisites

Renewing your Limited Liability Company (LLC) begins with acquainting yourself with your state's regulations. Usually, this information is available on your state's Secretary of State website or can be found by directly communicating with their office. This resource will highlight the forms, fees, and deadlines integral to the LLC renewal process.

Remember that each state prescribes its unique rules for LLC renewals. Consequently, these regulations can diverge concerning the process, the expenditure, and the submission deadlines. Ensure that you are well informed about the potential discrepancies between each state to evade the adverse impacts of non-adherence to these mandates.

Let us simplify this with an example, Delaware and Arizona. In Delaware, LLCs must remit an annual tax by the first day of June; however, an annual report is unnecessary. On the contrary, LLCs are exempt from an annual report or fee in Arizona unless they elect to be taxed as a corporation.

Update Your Information

With the requirements at your fingertips, you must assemble the necessary data. This usually demands an update of your LLC's details. Frequently updated details encompass:

- The official name of your LLC
- The primary office address
- The name and location of your registered agent
- Names and locations of the LLC's members or managers

Fill Out the Required Documents

Once you have collected all the essential data, your next step involves filling out the documents your state demands. This could be an *"Annual Report,"* a *"Statement of Information,"* or a document with a similar title. Depending on your state's preferred methods, you can complete this process online or by mail.

Pay the Filing Fee

Most states necessitate a filing fee for LLC renewal. The total could range significantly, from approximately $20 to several hundred dollars, contingent on the state. Confirm the fee amount and the acceptable payment methods with your state's business department or Secretary of State office.

Submit Your Renewal

The ultimate step is to send your forms and fee to the relevant state department. Pay heed to the deadline; some states require annual renewal, while others may have biennial requirements.

Business Licenses and Permits

Running a business involves numerous logistical and legal elements. One facet that you cannot overlook is the necessity of obtaining proper business licenses and permits. Every business requires certain licenses and permits to operate legally. These vary based on several factors, including the nature of your business, its location, and the specific regulations in place by local, state, and federal authorities.

Industry-Specific Licenses and Permits

Certain industries require specific licenses and permits due to the potential risks involved or the need to maintain certain standards of operation.

Take a restaurant, for instance. To operate a food service business, you will need a health department permit, a food handler's permit, and possibly a liquor license if you plan to serve alcohol. These permits ensure that your restaurant adheres to health and safety guidelines and complies with local and state laws around alcohol service.

In contrast, in running a construction company, you will need a building permit, zoning permit, or even a permit to dispose of hazardous waste, depending on the type of construction work involved. These licenses and permits show that your company is conducting business in a manner that is safe and minimally impactful to the environment and the community.

Location-Specific Requirements

These refer to the distinct licenses, permits, and certifications a business requires to operate legally within a specific jurisdiction. They are typically established and enforced by local or regional government bodies and can vary widely depending on the location. For example, a small retail store in New York City may require a city-specific business license, a sales tax permit, and a sign permit for their storefront. On the other hand, a similar store in a rural town in Ohio might not require a city-specific business license. However, it could still need a sales tax permit and a sign permit, depending on the local ordinances.

Obtaining and Renewing Licenses and Permits

Below is the process of obtaining and renewing these documents.

1. **Conduct Thorough Research**
   Start with a comprehensive research process to understand which licenses and permits are necessary for your business. Use resources like the U.S. Small Business Administration's *(SBA)* guide to federal business licenses and permits and your state's business licensing office for state-specific information.
2. **Apply for Licenses and Permits**
   Using the collected information, proceed with the application process. For instance, if you are opening a restaurant, you would consult with the local health department and apply for a food handler's permit. You might have to undergo necessary inspections to ensure your establishment meets health

and safety guidelines. Meanwhile, if your business operations have other elements, like serving alcohol at your restaurant, you may need additional permits. Applying for a liquor license often involves a comprehensive application process and possibly even community hearings.

3. **Keep Track of Validity and Expiration Dates**
   Remember, obtaining licenses and permits is not a one-time task. These documents usually have an expiry date and need to be renewed periodically to keep your business compliant with regulations. Once the validity of your permit is over, you must renew them. The renewal process can sometimes be as involved as the initial application. It generally requires a review of your business operations and compliance with any updated regulations.

General Tips

Having laid down the foundations, you now possess the essential knowledge to ensure your adherence to business regulations. Keeping track of numerous permits and reports can seem daunting and overwhelming. To assist you with this process, here are some valuable tips:

- **Anticipate Renewal Deadlines.** The deadlines for renewals have a way of creeping up on you. Therefore, it is prudent to set reminders for all your renewal deadlines to guarantee you do not overlook any.
- **Understand Zoning Laws.** To establish a physical location for your business, understand local zoning laws. These laws regulate land use and buildings within some geographical regions, specifying wheth-

er a zone is for residential, commercial, industrial, or mixed-use purposes. They can also stipulate specific details like building heights, subdivision of lands, parking requirements, and more.
- **Organize Your Documents.** Make sure you keep all your business documents, including licenses and permits, well-arranged. This will facilitate easier access to them when required, such as during the tax season or renewing your permits.
- **Factor Licensing and Permit Costs in Your Budget.** Remember to incorporate the cost of obtaining and renewing licenses and permits when drawing up your business budget. These are necessary expenses that can accumulate, particularly in certain industries.

Exercise: Staying Compliant as an LLC Owner

Here is an exercise to assist and motivate you in adhering to your legal responsibilities, such as filing reports and taxes, renewing your Limited Liability Company (LLC), and procuring the necessary business permits and licenses.

Gather the following items:

- A piece of paper
- A pen
- A calendar (either digital or physical)
- Access to the appropriate state or country regulations for LLCs, along with relevant tax information

Instructions:

1. **Comprehend Responsibilities.** Document all your legal obligations as an owner of an LLC on your paper. These obligations include filing reports and taxes, renewing your LLC, and securing business permits and licenses.
2. **Identify the Significance of Each Responsibility.** Articulate why each responsibility is crucial. The reasoning could include averting legal complications, avoiding financial penalties, maintaining a good relationship with the state, and contributing to a more efficiently functioning business.
3. **Fragmentation of Responsibilities.** Dissect each responsibility into smaller, more manageable tasks. For instance, filing taxes can be divided into monitoring expenses, totaling income, determining taxes due, and completing the required tax forms.
4. **Assign Deadlines.** With your calendar at the ready, designate due dates for each task. Utilize your state's or country's tax calendar and LLC renewal information as your references. Having visual reminders will aid in preventing any task from being overlooked.
5. **Set Reminders.** Use a digital calendar and activate automated reminders one or two weeks before each task's due date. This will allow you enough time to arrange and finish each job.
6. **Reward Yourself.** Compliance may not be the most exciting part of managing a business, so contemplate establishing rewards once you complete a task. This could include taking a break, indulging in your favorite treat, or investing time in a hobby.

Connecting these tasks to the broader advantages of your business and setting personal rewards can stimulate you to keep up with your legal duties as an owner of an LLC.

Chapter 8
Evaluating and Managing Risks

In the intricate weave of entrepreneurship, businesses, especially limited liability companies, face numerous risks. The onset of this reality is almost immediate from the moment the business starts. Navigating the economic tides, fluctuating market demands, and legal requirements is just the tip of the risk you may encounter. Grasping these potential threats by knowing the types of risks is the first step towards fortifying your business against potential catastrophes. This chapter will then guide you through the significance of risk assessment and other strategies for risk mitigation.

Types of Risks

While there are numerous types of risks, for the sake of simplification, they can be broadly classified into three main categories: *financial risk, operational risk, and reputational risk*. These categories encompass the primary challenges an LLC might encounter as it conducts its business operations.

Financial Risk

Financial risk is the possibility of experiencing losses resulting from financial events or decisions. The most common type of financial risk arises from the company's use of debt, known as leverage. If the company cannot generate enough revenue to meet its financial obligations, it may risk insolvency or bankruptcy.

For LLCs specifically, members could lose their investments in the business, though their assets would typically remain protected. Other aspects of financial risk may include **market risk** *(e.g., sudden market downturns, increased competition, changes in consumer behavior)*, **credit risk** *(e.g., non-payment by customers or clients)*, **liquidity risk** *(e.g., inability to access funds or convert assets into cash)*, and **inflation or foreign exchange risk**, especially if the LLC is operating or trading internationally.

Operational Risk

Operational risks are losses resulting from inadequate or failed processes, people, and systems or from external events. It includes anything from IT system failures, process breakdowns, fraud, human error, and even natural disasters. These risks can disrupt daily operations and negatively affect revenue. For example, a data breach due to inadequate cybersecurity measures could expose sensitive customer data, leading to financial penalties and decreased consumer trust. In an LLC that manufactures products, it is possible that machinery could fail, slowing the production and delivery of goods to customers.

Reputational Risk

The essence of reputational risk lies in the power of public opinion, capable of escalating any negative event associated with a company into a potentially damaging scenario. Such events could range from public scandals or controversial advertising campaigns to more subtle yet pervasive issues like poor customer service or lawsuits. The resonance of these situations within the public domain can significantly tarnish a company's image.

Furthermore, the stakes are even higher in LLCs. An adverse event can trigger a domino effect, leading to a loss in customer loyalty, increased regulatory scrutiny, or even legal complications. For instance, in 2015, Chipotle, the American fast-food chain, faced a series of foodborne illness outbreaks linked to E. coli, salmonella, and norovirus at several locations across the U.S. The incidents, widely reported in the media, led to a massive reputational crisis for Chipotle. Customers became wary, resulting in a significant decline in sales. Despite its efforts to rebuild consumer trust through improved food safety measures and marketing campaigns, the company's reputation suffered a severe blow. It took years for the company to recover its market position, illustrating the enduring impact of reputational risk on a business.

Risk Assessment

Different kinds of risks often intertwine. To simplify, consider this chain of events: A financial risk, like insufficient funds, might prevent a business from replacing an essential piece of machinery, creating an operational risk. The operational risk could then escalate into a reputational risk if the business cannot fulfill orders due to malfunctioning machinery. This situation can lead to customer dissatisfaction, resulting in bad reviews and damaging the company's reputation.

Therefore, effective risk management is vital for LLCs, which includes identifying, assessing, and controlling threats to the organization's capital and earnings. It typically involves creating a risk management plan and using strategies such as risk avoidance, reduction, sharing, and retention.

In essence, risk assessment is the compass that steers the ship of business strategy. It allows businesses to maneuver carefully, balancing the ambition to forge new paths with the caution of avoiding uncharted dangers.

Techniques for Managing Risks

Strategically managing business risks is a complex interplay of foresight, thoughtful planning, and adaptability. Yet, understand that completely eradicating all risks is not achievable. Thus, do not circumvent every risk. Instead, forge a resilient business that can persist and prosper amidst challenges. Here are three key strategies:

- **Risk Avoidance.** Sometimes, the best way to handle risk is to avoid risky activities. However, it must be used judiciously, as it often involves foregoing potential opportunities.
- **Risk Reduction.** Minimize the impact of a risk, often by implementing safeguards or fallback plans. For example, an LLC could establish an emergency fund to offset financial risks or diversify suppliers to mitigate operational risks.
- **Risk Transfer.** There are occasions when risks can be shifted to another party. This strategy is often implemented through contracts or insurance. For an LLC, insurance policies can be a lifeline. It protects the business from potentially devastating financial losses and serves as a financial shield against unexpected calamities.

Insurance Types

Running an LLC involves facing an array of risks. Nonetheless, having the right insurance coverage will help your LLC mitigate potential financial losses from unforeseen circumstances.

The types and amounts of insurance needed can vary greatly depending on the nature of your LLC, its size, location, and industry. Consult with an experienced insurance broker or legal advisor to make sure you have adequate coverage for your specific needs. Remember, being proactive with your insurance decisions can help in the long-term sustainability and growth of your LLC as it helps lessen the risk it faces.

Here are some types of insurance that your LLC might need to consider:

General Liability Insurance

General Liability Insurance, or Commercial General Liability *(CGL)*, is a vital business policy. It protects your business from financial loss should your company be found legally responsible for damage caused to third parties, such as bodily injury, property damage, or even advertising injury.

Professional Liability Insurance

Errors and Omissions *(E&O)* insurance or Professional Liability Insurance is designed to protect your LLC from potential financial loss arising from claims of negligence or failure to provide the level of advice or service your clients expect. This insurance type is particularly pertinent for PLLCs that offer professional services or advice.

Property Insurance

Consider having property insurance if your LLC owns or leases physical spaces, like offices or retail locations. As such, it covers damage to or loss of business property due to events like fires, storms, theft, and other covered perils.

Cyber Liability Insurance

In the digital age, data breaches and cyber threats are ever-present risks. If your LLC handles sensitive customer data *(credit card information, personal data, etc.)*, consider Cyber Liability Insurance. This coverage helps manage the costs associated with data breaches, including notification costs, credit monitoring services, and fines or penalties.

Business Interruption Insurance

Business Interruption Insurance, or Business Income Insurance, compensates for lost income during events that disrupt the normal operation of your business, such as natural disasters. It can help cover operating expenses and lost revenue during the interruption.

Financing Growth

Business is frequently gauged by growth— the enlargement of market share, diversification of product offerings, and revenue increment, among other factors. However, the growth journey is filled with financial obstacles that necessitate strategic planning and brave decision-making. In this context, the conversation about risk assessment and management becomes paramount, as comprehending and alleviating risks form the foundation for sustainable growth. Remembering that successful risk management directly impacts a company's readiness for growth is essential.

Having emphasized the importance of risk management, we should now shift our focus to financing growth. This section will delve into the expansive world of growth financing, exploring the many options available to businesses aspiring to fund their expansion.

Reinvestment of Profits

Growing a business is akin to nurturing a garden. Generated profits are the water and sunlight needed for your business to flourish. These profits can be viewed in two ways. As such, they either be distributed as dividends among the shareholders, or they can be reinvested back into the business—*much like a gardener using the seeds from his crops to grow even more plants.*

Reinvestment of profits also called plowing back of profits, is a strategic decision businesses make aiming for long-term growth. These funds can be reinvested into various areas such as product development, research, and development, marketing, workforce expansion, or upgrading infrastructure and technology. The primary objective is to create more value and, in turn, generate higher profits.

This strategy requires a careful balancing act. On the one hand, shareholders may demand dividends, especially if the company is consistently profitable. Conversely, reinvestment could potentially lead to increased future profits and a rise in share price, which would also benefit shareholders.

Amazon's Strategy for Reinvesting Profits

A classic example of a company that has heavily relied on the reinvestment of profits to fuel its growth is Amazon. Since its inception in 1994, Amazon has reinvested its profits into various areas of its business to expand its reach, improve its services, and create a long-term competitive advantage.

In its initial years, Amazon was just an online bookseller. However, instead of distributing its profits, Amazon continually reinvested in expanding its product categories, eventually becoming the *"one-stop shop."* Subsequently, the company invested profits in developing technologies and services like *Kindle, Amazon Web Services, Prime Membership, and Alexa*. These investments have not only diversified Amazon's revenue streams but also solidified its position as a leader in e-commerce and technology.

Even though this aggressive reinvestment strategy meant Amazon rarely posted a profit and did not pay dividends to its shareholders in its early years, its stock continued to rise. Investors saw value in Amazon's relentless focus on expansion and customer service. In the present day, Amazon stands as one of the world's most valuable companies. Its share price is now worth more than a hundred dollars. This value represents an astounding increase from its initial public offering price of $18 *(adjusted for splits)* in 1997.

Loans or Investments

While reinvestment of profits is a sound strategy, it may not always be sufficient, especially for ambitious expansion plans. In such instances, businesses often turn to external financing sources, such as loans or investments. Regardless, below is how loans and investments are used in growing your business.

Securing a business loan from a bank or a financial institution is a common method of financing growth. However, loans come with the obligation of repayment, often with interest, which businesses should factor into their financial planning.

Alternatively, businesses can explore securing additional investments to finance their growth. This approach differs significantly from taking out a loan. Instead of repaying a borrowed sum with interest, businesses offer a stake in their company's equity to these investors, as discussed in an earlier chapter. In effect, these investors become part-owners of the business. On a positive note, investors often bring their expertise and networks to the table, which can be invaluable assets as the company navigates its growth trajectory. In return, the investors share in the potential future success of the business, making it a mutually beneficial relationship.

The capital influx from investors and loans can fund various expansion activities such as research and development, acquiring other businesses, scaling production, boosting marketing efforts, or hiring key talents.

Chipotle's Rapid Expansion Due to External Investments

For instance, a real-world example would be the case of Chipotle Mexican Grill. Chipotle, a well-known fast-food chain focusing on burritos and tacos, started as a single restaurant in Denver, Colorado, in 1993. The founder, Steve Ells, had a simple yet ambitious idea of providing fast food that did not compromise quality.

Ells' concept caught the attention of McDonald's Corporation, which saw potential in the budding chain. In 1998, McDonald's invested significantly in Chipotle, becoming a majority stakeholder. This investment gave the company the financial backing to rapidly expand its operations.

Over the next eight years, Chipotle grew from just 16 locations to over 500 across the country, with McDonald's investment playing a crucial role in this aggressive expansion. In 2006, Chipotle went public, and McDonald's divested its investment, but the growth did not stop there. As of 2021, it has over 2,700 locations globally.

This example showcases how securing significant external investment can fuel an ambitious growth strategy. Likewise, it shows how strategic financial partnerships can catapult a business to new heights.

Mergers and Acquisitions

Mergers and acquisitions *(M&A)* are strategic decisions taken by businesses aiming to expand their operational horizon, reach new markets, increase their portfolio, or simply stay ahead of the competition. This growth path also comes with complexities, but the potential rewards often outweigh the risks.

M&A can take on several forms. A merger typically happens between companies of roughly equal size that decide to continue as a single, larger entity. The goal is often to consolidate resources, share expertise, and expand the customer base. On the other hand, an acquisition involves a larger company purchasing a smaller one. The smaller company becomes a larger entity, often enhancing its product or service offerings.

Disney's Acquisition of Pixar

One notable example of successful growth through acquisition is the Walt Disney Company's purchase of Pixar Animation Studios in 2006.

Pixar, known for its groundbreaking technology and creative storytelling, had been in a successful distribution partnership with Disney for years, producing hits like *"Toy Story"* and *"Finding Nemo."* However, tensions between the two companies started to rise, and it seemed like Pixar would seek a new partner.

Walt Disney wanted to blend its distinct film style with Pixar's outstanding storytelling methods. Seeing the potential in Pixar's unique capabilities and the risk of losing them to a competitor, Disney decided to buy Pixar for $7.4 billion. This strategic acquisition not only kept Pixar's innovative technology and creative prowess within Disney's fold but also opened up new avenues for Disney's animation division.

This success was not without challenges. The two companies had distinct corporate cultures—Pixar's culture was built on creativity and innovation, while Disney was known for its traditional, hierarchical structure. Yet, Disney handled the integration well, preserving Pixar's culture and operating style and allowing Pixar's leadership to influence Disney's animation division.

Today, the acquisition is considered a resounding success. Pixar continues to produce blockbuster films, contributing significantly to Disney's revenue and reputation as a leading player in the animation industry. Furthermore, it has reinforced Disney's brand image, diversified its movie portfolio, and led to significant cost efficiencies and increased market penetration.

Exercise: Design a Risk Management Plan

This activity will help you put the lessons of this chapter into practice.

Objective:
Design a risk management plan for a hypothetical LLC in a field of your choice. This plan will help you understand the complexities of risk management and appreciate its role in safeguarding a company's assets and ensuring its growth.

Instructions:

1. **Identify the Business.** Begin by defining your hypothetical LLC. Describe its nature, industry, size, and operating location.
2. **Categorize Risks.** Identify potential financial, operational, and reputational risks your business might face. Try to list at least three potential risks in each category.
3. **Risk Evaluation.** Analyze the identified risks. Assess the likelihood of each risk occurring and the potential impact it would have on your business. This could be quantified in financial terms or metrics like customer satisfaction or brand image.

4. **Mitigation Strategies.** Develop strategies to manage each risk. These strategies can include risk avoidance, mitigation, or transfer. Be specific about the steps your business could take to implement these strategies.
5. **Insurance Coverage.** Decide on the types of insurance that would be beneficial for your LLC. Justify your choices based on the identified risks.
6. **Growth Financing.** Design a strategic plan for financing your business's growth. As such, it includes reinvesting profits, seeking loans or investments, or considering mergers and acquisitions.
7. **Review and Refine.** Take a step back and review your entire risk management plan. Consider if there is any area that needs more attention or any additional risks that need to be accounted for.

Although this exercise is designed for a hypothetical LLC, you can adapt the principles learned here to real-world scenarios.

LLCs face financial, operational, and reputational risks requiring effective management and appropriate insurance coverage, including property, cyber liability, and business interruption insurance. Business growth can be achieved through reinvesting profits, like Amazon, or securing external financing, like Chipotle. Mergers and acquisitions, as in Disney's case, provide expansion opportunities. Constructing a risk management plan, considering insurance needs, and strategizing growth financing are pivotal for understanding business growth and risk management complexities.

Chapter 9
Exit Strategies

Running a limited liability company is a monumental task with its fair share of ups and downs. As you navigate through the business landscape, continually innovating, growing, and facing challenges head-on, there comes a time when you may ponder over the next significant step: *the exit strategy.*

An **exit strategy** is a component of your business blueprint right from the beginning. It provides a roadmap for what to do when stepping back from the business due to retirement, a change in personal circumstances, or simply because you are ready for your next venture. A well-planned exit strategy can ensure that you exit on your terms while maximizing the value of your business.

This chapter explores three major exit strategies for your LLC: *Selling your business, merging it with another or having it acquired, and dissolving it entirely.* Likewise, there is information about the consideration for each strategy, how to implement them, and the steps to ensure compliance with laws and respect for all stakeholders involved.

Reasons to Consider Crafting an Exit Strategy

The following are reasons why an exit strategy might be the necessary step in your business journey.

- **Personal Reasons.** Over time, your circumstances or ambitions may change. You might be eyeing retirement, wishing to spend more time with family, or exploring new opportunities or passions. An exit strategy provides a clear path to transition from your business when personal changes arise.
- **Financial Security.** Selling your LLC or merging it with another business can be profitable, allowing you to reap the financial rewards of the hard work and dedication you've poured into your business.
- **Business Performance.** If your business is not performing as expected or has consistently been incurring losses, it might be time to consider an exit. Dissolving the business might be tough, but it could be the best way to mitigate further financial damage.
- **Market Changes.** At times, market or industry shifts can profoundly influence your business. Factors such as technological evolution, the emergence of new competitors, shifts in customer tastes, or regulatory amendments can potentially undermine the viability of your current business model. It may be more appropriate to withdraw in a planned and orderly fashion by having an exit strategy in response to these.
- **Succession Planning.** If you have no successors in line or if your successors are not ready or willing to take over, an exit strategy provides a way to ensure

that your business continues to thrive after your departure.
- **Risk Management.** Owning a business comes with inherent risks. Over time, as you accumulate personal wealth, the risk associated with your business could become disproportionate to your potential return. In such cases, executing an exit strategy can be a prudent move in terms of risk management and safeguarding your financial stability.

Types of Exit Strategies

Every business owner's situation and goals are unique, and your exit strategy should reflect your circumstances and ambitions. A thoughtfully planned exit strategy helps you conclude one chapter of your entrepreneurial journey and smoothly transition to the next.

Selling Your LLC

As the owner of a limited liability company. you put in countless hours and immeasurable effort into building your business. However, there may come a time when you decide to embark on a new journey or take a step back from the business world. In such instances, selling your LLC becomes a prominent choice, providing a path that allows for new opportunities while benefiting from the value you created in your business. This route allows you to reap the financial rewards of your hard work and dedication, converting the value you've built into a tangible payoff.

Selling your LLC necessitates not just finding the right buyer but also accurately valuing your business and navigating a maze of financial, legal, and procedural details. This section aims to guide you through selling your LLC, providing insights into valuing your business and explaining the key steps in a successful sale.

Valuation of an LLC

Valuing an LLC can be challenging, especially for small businesses, as there isn't a one-size-fits-all approach. Several factors come into play, including the business's financial health, industry trends, market position, and potential for future growth.

One common method for valuation is the **earnings multiplier method**, which takes the company's net income and multiplies it by a certain factor, usually dictated by industry standards. For example, if your LLC had an annual net income of $100 thousand and the industry-standard multiplier was 5, the estimated value would be $500 thousand.

However, remember that no business operates in isolation. Therefore, you must consider the macroeconomic conditions and industry health when using the earnings multiplier method. For instance, in a struggling economy or a declining industry, potential buyers may be unwilling to pay a high multiplier.

Another popular method is the **discounted cash flow (DCF) analysis**. This method estimates the company's value based on future cash flows. DCF analysis considers the time value of money— the idea that a dollar today is worth more than a dollar tomorrow. The downside is that DCF analysis relies heavily on future projections, which can be uncertain.

Lastly, the **asset-based valuation method** could be employed. values the LLC based on the total value of its assets minus liabilities. Often, it is used for companies with significant physical assets like real estate or equipment. However, it does not account for intangible assets like goodwill or brand value.

Process for Selling Your LLC

This significant transition requires you to navigate through a variety of stages. To ensure the successful sale of your LLC, do the following:

1. **Prepare Your Business for Sale.** Ensure your business is ready for sale. This includes streamlining financial records, strengthening customer relationships, and resolving pending operational issues. During this phase, you should also determine the valuation of your LLC.
2. **Identify Potential Buyers.** The next step is to seek potential buyers. As such, it could be competitors, other companies in your industry, or even your employees. Engaging a business broker can be beneficial at this stage as they can access a broader network of potential buyers and negotiate terms on your behalf.
3. **Negotiate Terms of Sale.** With potential buyers in the picture, the negotiation process begins. This is when your business valuation and financial projections become critical. Be ready to defend your valuation, keeping in mind that buyers are not just purchasing your existing business but also its future potential.

4. **Perform Due Diligence.** After settling on terms, the due diligence phase ensues. In this stage, the buyer thoroughly examines the LLC's financial and operational detail to confirm that everything is as represented.
5. **Draft and Sign a Sales Agreement.** Create a sales agreement that outlines the terms of the sale and effectuates the transfer of the LLC ownership. Involving legal counsel is crucial here to ensure the legal validity of the agreement and compliance with all necessary conditions.

Mergers and Acquisitions

Mergers and acquisitions are often considered a strategy for growth or consolidation in business. However, they can also serve as a viable and strategic exit option.

For instance, **merging** involves melding two distinct business entities, each with its culture, operations, and vision. On the other hand, **acquisition** involves another company taking over your LLC, often with the intention of harnessing your business's unique capabilities or market position to augment its operations. Such a transaction could offer increased market share, diversification, cost efficiencies, and potentially even a lucrative financial return for you.

Effects of Mergers and Acquisitions

Navigating a merger or acquisition requires careful planning, negotiation, and due diligence to ensure a smooth transition and preserve the value of your business. Despite the complexities, these strategies can open doors to new opportunities and serve as a fruitful culmination of your journey as an LLC owner.

Market Expansion

Expanding market reach is one of their significant advantages. Your LLC can gain access to new customers, markets, or geographic areas that were previously inaccessible. For instance, if your LLC specializes in crafting artisanal cheese in New York, merging with a business in California could allow your products to reach a broader audience without the hassle of establishing a new operation from scratch.

Resource Combination

This refers not just to financial resources but also to human capital, technology, intellectual property, and infrastructure. If your LLC has developed advanced technologies or accumulated substantial intellectual property, a merger or being acquired by a business with robust marketing resources could maximize the value of these assets. Conversely, if your business has been struggling to develop certain capabilities, being acquired by a company that possesses these could fill the gap.

Profitability Enhancement

Mergers and acquisitions often result in improved profitability. This can happen through increased revenue from the broader market reach and the potential for cost savings through economies of scale. Aside from this, redundant operations can be streamlined, excess facilities can be eliminated, and administrative functions can be consolidated, leading to significant cost savings and improved operational efficiency.

The Process of Mergers or Acquisitions

Acquisition or merging with another business involves several steps, each requiring careful thought and planning. Its goal is to ensure a smooth transition and achieve the envisioned benefits of the M&A. With thoughtful planning and execution, the integration phase can lead to a powerful business entity ready to conquer new heights.

1. **Identify Potential Partners or Acquirers.** The first step in any merger or acquisition process is identifying potential partners or acquirers. This could be a business in the same industry, a complementary one, or even a supplier or customer. The vital aspect here is to seek a business that aligns with your company's vision, culture, and strategic objectives. For instance, a health-focused restaurant chain may find a perfect partner in a company offering fitness programs and services. Their joint vision of promoting healthier lifestyles could make for a powerful combined entity.
2. **Negotiate Terms.** Once a potential partner or acquirer is identified, the negotiation phase begins. Here, the terms of the merger or acquisition are decided, including the structure of the new business entity, division of ownership, and roles of the existing owners in the post-M&A company. Entering negotiations with a clear understanding of your expectations in terms of financial gains and future role is crucial. This clarity helps in laying down your terms firmly and making well-informed decisions.
3. **Conduct Due Diligence.** After successful negotiations, the due diligence process commences. This critical stage involves a comprehensive examination

of the potential partner's financial records, contracts, business operations, and other relevant information. The purpose is to uncover potential risks or liabilities that could impact the new entity formed post-merger or acquisition. For instance, discovering unresolved legal issues or significant debt during due diligence could potentially influence the terms of the M&A or even halt the process altogether.

4. **Integrate the Businesses.** The final stage is the integration of the two businesses. This phase involves harmonizing the operations, cultures, and strategies of the two companies into a cohesive whole. Usually, it is the most challenging phase, requiring strategic change management and clear communication with all stakeholders. Likewise, it involves merging HR policies, harmonizing technological systems, aligning marketing strategies, or even finding a common corporate language if the businesses are from different cultural backgrounds.

Dissolution

Dissolving an LLC signifies bringing your business to an end in a formal, legally compliant manner. While it might seem like a grim prospect, there could be circumstances when dissolving your LLC is the most prudent decision. Even if it is prompted by continuous financial losses, insurmountable legal issues, shifting market dynamics, or personal circumstances, dissolution is an exit strategy that deserves consideration.

Many confuse dissolution with liquidation. To clear the air, they are both means to an end, but they approach this end differently. **Dissolution** is a broader, more formal process that legally ends a business entity's existence. It is typically initiated by the company's owners and involves satisfying all outstanding obligations, including the liquidation of assets if necessary.

On the other hand, **liquidation** specifically refers to the process of converting a company's assets to cash to settle outstanding debts. As such, it was necessitated by insolvency and is often managed by an appointed liquidator.

Thus, dissolution could encompass liquidation. Yet, liquidation could be a standalone process without resulting in the dissolution of the company, especially in cases of partial liquidation or as part of restructuring efforts.

Steps to Dissolving Your LLC

Dissolving an LLC requires more than merely stopping business activities. This action must adhere to state laws and regulations, and it generally consists of several steps.

1. **Decide on the Dissolution.** Decide collectively as a company to halt operations. This crucial decision should involve all the company's members, and depending on the terms of your LLC's operating agreement, it may demand a majority vote or unanimous consent. Keep a formal written record of this decision-making process, noting the time and method of the vote.
2. **Address Outstanding Liabilities.** The subsequent stage concerns the settlement of all remaining liabilities. This may entail settling business debts, resolving

any ongoing legal issues, and completing any unfulfilled contractual commitments. Should the LLC lack sufficient resources to satisfy all its debts, adhere to your state law's stipulations regarding the order of repaying creditors. It might be necessary to liquidate business assets to fulfill these financial responsibilities.

3. **Submit Articles of Dissolution.** After all financial and legal commitments have been settled, the next stage is to officially terminate your LLC by submitting the articles of dissolution. This submission should be made to your state's Secretary of State or a similar governing body. Given that the procedures and fees associated with filing may vary, it's crucial to familiarize yourself with your specific state's regulations.

4. **Communicate with Relevant Stakeholders.** The concluding step in the dissolution procedure involves notifying all pertinent parties about the LLC's dissolution. This group generally consists of creditors, clients, suppliers, employees, and any other entities that maintained a professional affiliation with your company.

Deciding the Best Exit Strategy

Choosing the right exit strategy for your Limited Liability Company *(LLC)* is a decision that requires careful contemplation and a keen understanding of your business, personal ambitions, and market dynamics. Each strategy has its unique considerations, advantages, and challenges. Making the right choice can help ensure a smooth transition and a rewarding end to your entrepreneurial journey.

One could liken the decision to choosing a path in a dense, enchanted forest. Each path offers a different adventure with its unique allure and challenges. The key is to choose the path that aligns best with your business goals and personal circumstances.

Selling your LLC is like opting for the path of golden treasures. It provides the opportunity to monetize the value you've built in your business, yielding financial rewards that could support your next venture or secure your retirement. In fact, it is an enticing path if your business is profitable, has a unique value proposition, and there's a clear market of potential buyers. However, this path requires careful navigation: *valuing your business accurately, finding the right buyer, and managing a complex selling process.*

Integrating your LLC with another business through mergers and acquisitions is akin to choosing the path of powerful alliances. This path offers the prospect of combining strengths, resources, and market reach with another entity, creating a business that's potentially stronger and more competitive. This could be an ideal route if your business complements another or if a merger could unlock new market opportunities or operational efficiencies. However, it requires finding a compatible partner and going through the complex integration process while preserving the best of both entities.

Meanwhile, **dissolving your LLC** is like choosing the path of graceful endings. It involves formally closing down your business, ceasing operations, and settling all obligations. This path could be the most prudent if your business is consistently losing money, is faced with insurmountable challenges, or if personal circumstances require a complete exit. While it might seem like a path of retreat, it can also be a path of responsibility and wisdom, allowing you to limit further losses and possibly pave the way for a fresh start.

Remember, there is no universal *'best'* path— only the path that is best for you, given your unique circumstances, goals, and aspirations. As you stand at this crossroads, take the time to reflect, seek advice, and listen to your instincts. Remember that each path, while marked by the promise of the destination, also offers an adventure in itself— the process of selling, the journey of merging and being acquired, or the wisdom in dissolving.

Exercise: What is Your Ideal Exit Strategy?

Answer the following questions truthfully and tally your answers to know which exit strategy aligns with your current business and personal situation.

1. What is your primary motivation for exiting your business?
    a. I want to explore other opportunities or ventures.
    b. I want to leverage the company's value and generate high returns.
    c. I need to mitigate further financial losses.
    d. I am retiring or unable to continue running the business.
2. How would you describe the current financial health of your business?
    a. The business is profitable with robust growth prospects.

      b. I have a steady revenue stream, but growth has plateaued.

      c. Our business is struggling financially.

      d. I have considerable debt that exceeds my income.

3. What is the status of successors in your business?

      a. I have identified potential successors who are keen to take over.

      b. There are no successors, but I believe the company can still thrive under new leadership.

      c. I am unsure about potential successors or their willingness to take over.

      d. There are no successors and the business may struggle to survive without current leadership.

4. How do you view your business's market position and future growth prospects?

      a. We have a strong market position with promising growth potential.

      b. Our market position is stable, but growth prospects are moderate.

      c. We are losing our market position due to intense competition or market changes.

      d. Our market position is deteriorating, and future growth looks uncertain.

5. How do you see the operational continuity of your business without you?

      a. The business can run smoothly without my involvement.

      b. The business might face some challenges, but it can still function.

      c. The business may struggle to maintain its operations without me.

d. The business will likely collapse without my involvement.

Quiz Results:

- **Mostly As:** Selling your LLC. Your business is in a healthy state with promising growth potential. Selling could provide high returns and free you to explore other opportunities.
- **Mostly Bs:** Mergers and Acquisitions. Your business performs adequately but needs a new strategic direction to unlock growth potential. Merging with or being acquired by another entity could provide synergistic benefits and elevate your company's market position.
- **Mostly Cs**: Exit and Start a New Venture. Your business faces significant challenges, and you might benefit from exploring new opportunities. Consider finding a potential buyer for your business or starting anew in a different market or industry.
- **Mostly Ds:** Dissolving your LLC. Your business is under severe financial stress, and it might not survive without your involvement. Winding up the business could prevent further financial losses and free up your resources for future ventures.

Exercise: Crafting Your Exit Strategy Plan

This exercise will guide you through the early stages of planning your exit strategy. It is designed to get you thinking about your LLC's future, your options, and the steps you need to take to make your chosen exit strategy a reality.

Instructions:

1. **Reflect on your long-term goals.** Start by writing down your personal long-term goals and ambitions. *Are you hoping to retire at a certain age? Do you have another business idea you want to pursue? Or are you aiming to pass your business down to a family member?* Write these down in as much detail as possible.
2. **Consider your exit options.** *Based on your long-term goals, which exit strategy seems to be the most suitable for you now? Selling, merging, acquiring, or dissolving your LLC?* Write down your chosen exit strategy and explain why you believe it is your best choice.
3. **Valuation.** If you are considering selling or merging your LLC or having it acquired by another business, *how would you go about valuing it? What assets, both tangible and intangible, do you think add the most value to your business?* List these and provide a tentative valuation if possible.
4. **Potential Buyers or Partners.** *Whom would you consider as potential buyers or partners? Why?*
5. **Next Steps.** *What immediate steps must you take toward implementing your chosen exit strategy?* This may involve speaking to a business broker, initiating a business valuation, or discussing your plans with a business partner or family member. Be as specific as possible with these steps.

A successful exit strategy involves careful thought, planning, and expert advice. Be sure to consult with professionals as you further develop your plan.

Conclusion

Wrapping up this all-inclusive guide involves connecting the various components that comprise the creation, operation, and dissolution of a Limited Liability Company (LLC). This journey began with a thorough examination of the LLC concept and structure, moving to cover topics like formation procedures, financial considerations, ownership roles and responsibilities, taxation, compliance, growth planning, and concluding with exit strategies.

Central to this narrative is the understanding that mastering the complex aspects of establishing and managing an LLC is crucial to its successful operation. This guide aims to deliver a detailed, easy-to-understand manual that helps navigate the complexities of setting up and operating an LLC, avoiding common pitfalls, and establishing a robust foundation for an entrepreneurial journey.

The **LLC formation process** is a carefully structured procedure that begins with naming the business and selecting a registered agent, followed by filing the articles of organization. This process is vital to set the right tone for the business and ensure its legality.

Financing is a significant part of running an LLC, and this guide has illuminated different options ranging from self-funding to loans, grants, and seeking investors. Beyond financing, this guide has explored the critical role of an LLC owner, which includes decision-making and record-keeping.

Understanding **taxation and maintaining compliance** are key to managing an LLC; failing to grasp these components could have severe consequences. This guide has provided an in-depth discussion about the tax advantages and disadvantages of an LLC, the importance of hiring a tax professional, regular reporting, business licenses, and permits.

A successful LLC also requires **growth planning and risk management**. This guide has offered insights into various types of risks, the importance of insurance, and strategies to finance growth. The discussion concluded with exit strategies, whether that involves selling, merging, being acquired, or dissolving the LLC.

Likewise, operating an LLC is a complex, multi-faceted task that demands careful planning, continuous learning, and adaptability. While this guide offers a comprehensive overview, it is important to remember that every business is unique, and professional advice should always be sought to navigate specific circumstances.

This guide has served as an insightful, useful resource, providing the clarity and understanding necessary for forming, managing, and maintaining an LLC. The content of the book is there for revisiting whenever required. May this guide empower you to take the path toward business success, turning the entrepreneurial vision into a tangible reality.

Glossary

Agreement. A contract or understanding reached between two or more parties.

Business Entity. An organization formed to conduct business. It may be a corporation, a partnership, a Limited Liability Company (LLC), or another structure.

Company. A commercial enterprise, a business, or a firm. It can be an umbrella term for various types of business entities.

Dissolution. The process of closing or terminating a business entity's existence.

Equity. Ownership interest in a business, represented by shares in a corporation or membership interests in an LLC.

Franchise. A legal and commercial relationship between the owner of a trademark, brand, or business model (the franchisor) and an individual or company (the franchisee) authorized to operate using the franchisor's brand or model.

Liability. The state of being responsible for something, especially by law; in business, it refers to financial debts or obligations.

Management. Dealing with or controlling things or people within a business entity.

Operating Agreement. A key document used by LLCs because it outlines the business' financial and functional decisions, including rules, regulations, and provisions.

Partnership. A type of business entity where two or more individuals share ownership, with each partner contributing to all aspects of the business.

Registered Agent. A business or individual designated to receive service of process when a business entity is a party in a legal action.

Sole Proprietorship. A type of enterprise owned and run by one individual and in which there is no legal distinction between the owner and the business entity.

Taxation. The means by which governments finance their expenditure by imposing charges on citizens and corporate entities.

Venture Capital. A type of private equity financing that investors provide to startup companies and small businesses that are believed to have long-term growth potential.

Withdrawal. The action of removing something, especially money. In business, it refers to taking money from a business by its owners.

Yield. The income return on an investment, such as the interest or dividends received from holding a particular security.

Zoning. A device of land use planning used by local governments, which involves dividing land into zones where various uses are permitted.

Resources

Aaron Sanders. 'DIY Guide to Forming Your Own LLC.' A Detail Step-by-Step Guide to Starting and Filing a Limited Liability Company for All 50 States and DC, CreateSpace Independent Publishing Platform, 2018

Anthony Mancuso. 'Nolo's Quick LLC.' All You Need to Know About Limited Liability Companies (Quick & Legal), NOLO, 2015

Disney Pixar Merger Case Study. StudySmarter UK. https://www.studysmarter.co.uk/explanations/business-studies/business-case-studies/disney-pixar-merger-case-study/#:~:text=Walt%20Disney%20purchased%20Pixar%20company,corporate%20transactions%20in%20recent%20years. n.d.

Eloise Skinner. 'The Purpose Handbook.' A beginner's guide to figuring out what you're here to do, Practical Inspiration Publishing, 2021

Evans, B. (2021). Why Amazon Has No Profits — Benedict Evans. Benedict Evans. https://www.ben-evans.com/benedictevans/2014/why-amazon-has-no-profits-and-why-it-works

Hart, K. The Chipotle Guacamole Hack That Changes Everything. Mashed. https://www.mashed.com/230872/

the-chipotle-guacamole-hack-that-changes-everything/ 2020

Hay, H. Disney To Acquire Pixar - The Walt Disney Company. The Walt Disney Company. https://thewaltdisneycompany.com/disney-to-acquire-pixar/ 2018

Ingo Walter. 'Mergers and Acquisitions in Banking and Finance.' What Works, what Fails, and why, Oxford University Press, 2004

Jennifer Reuting. 'Limited Liability Companies For Dummies.' John Wiley & Sons, 2019

Lécia Vicente. 'The Law and Economics of Restrictions on Transfer of Shares.' Taming Property Rights in Shares and the Silver Fox, SSRN, 2015

MaBgorzata AatuszyDska. 'Decision-Making in Management.' Methods and Behavioral Tools, Kesra Nermend, Springer Nature, 2021

Marves, C. Food Poisoning at Chipotle | A History of Food Safety Issues. Food Poisoning News. https://www.foodpoisoningnews.com/food-poisoning-at-chipotle-a-history-of-food-safety-issues/ 2022

Michael McCann. 'Record-keeping and Reporting Requirements.' OSHA-PESH, 1999

Mike Michalowicz. 'Profit First.' Transform Your Business from a Cash-Eating Monster to a Money-Making Machine, Penguin, 2017

Molly F. Sherlock. 'The Corporate Income Tax System.' Overview and Options for Reform, Mark P. Keightley, CreateSpace Independent Publishing Platform, 2012

Robert A. Cooke. 'How to Start Your Own 'S' Corporation.' Wiley, 2001

Robert J. Mintz. 'Asset Protection for Physicians and High-Risk Business Owners.' Robert J Mintz, 2010

Schuyler B. Jackson. 'Rational Meaning.' A New Foundation for the Definition of Words and Supplementary Essays, Laura (Riding) Jackson, University of Virginia Press, 1997

Shamsu Yahaya. 'Does the operator in a Joint Operating Agreement owe a fiduciary duty to non-operators?.' A case study of the USA Model Forms and judicial decisions, GRIN Verlag, 2010

The Florida Bar Continuing Legal Education. 'Asset Protection in Florida.' LexisNexis, 2015

Vernon R. Proctor. 'Drafting Delaware Limited Liability Company Agreements.' Forms and Practice Manual, John M. Cunningham, Wolters Kluwer, 2009

Vernon R. Proctor. 'Drafting Limited Liability Company Operating Agreements, Fourth Edition.' John M. Cunningham, Wolters Kluwer, 2016

Viviane Simon-Brown. 'Choosing Your Group's Structure, Mission, and Goals.' Oregon State University Extension Service, 1999

Wallace "Wally" J. Schupbach. 'Introduction to Making Decisions.' Xlibris Corporation, 2010

Exclusive Bonuses

Dear Reader,

I'm excited to share with you two exclusive bonuses that I've curated to complement your journey in understanding and managing Limited Liability Companies.

- **Bonus 1: Marketing and Branding Ideas for Your LLC:** A comprehensive guide offering innovative marketing and branding strategies to enhance your LLC's market presence and build a strong brand identity.
- **Bonus 2: Resources and Tools for Your LLC Success:** A curated collection of essential tools and resources designed to streamline operations, manage finances, and boost the productivity of your LLC.

How to Access Your Bonuses:

Scan the QR Code Below: Simply use your phone's camera or a QR code reader to scan the code, and you'll be directed straight to the bonus content.

Visit the Link: You can also access these valuable resources by visiting https://bit.ly/Martin-LLC

Embark on a Successful LLC Journey!

I am confident that these bonuses will enrich your understanding and assist you in navigating the exciting world of LLCs. Thank you for joining me on this journey.

Warm regards,

Carolyn Ava Martin

Made in United States
Troutdale, OR
06/11/2024

20455940R00096